A Message From Verizon

You might be wondering what does Verizon have to do with dining out, shopping and enjoying free time in lower Manhattan?

A lot, actually. Because lower Manhattan is our neighborhood, too. It's where Verizon offers service and where many of us live and work. We're committed to getting lower Manhattan back to business and stronger than ever after the September 11th tragedy. That's why we're proud to sponsor this *Zagat Downtown New York City Survey*.

We hope this guide encourages you to come down to have a meal. Do some shopping. Take in a museum. Stay in a hotel. Or whatever else you can do to give this vital part of Manhattan a much-needed boost. As a resident of this neighborhood, I have seen firsthand how these local businesses have been affected. That's why I personally urge you to do whatever you can to help turn things around.

We at Verizon would also like to take this opportunity to thank our customers. Your business is greatly appreciated. You can always count on us to be there for you. Together, we know our city will come through this time of crisis stronger than ever.

Thanks for your support,

[signature]

Bruce S. Gordon
President-Retail Market Groups, Verizon

Y0-AID-860

ZAGATSURVEY
SPECIAL EDITION

DOWNTOWN NEW YORK CITY

Editors: Curt Gathje, Carol Diuguid and Laura Mitchell

Coordinator: Larry Cohn

Published and distributed by
ZAGAT SURVEY, LLC
4 Columbus Circle
New York, New York 10019
Tel: 212 977 6000
E-mail: TK@zagat.com
Web site: www.zagat.com

Acknowledgments

This guide would not have been possible without the hard work of our staff, especially Betsy Andrews, Deirdre Bourdet, Phil Cardone, Reni Chin, Anne Cole, Erica Curtis, Jessica Fields, Jeff Freier, Shelley Gallagher, Randi Gollin, Jessica Gonzalez, Diane Karlin, Natalie Lebert, Mike Liao, Dave Makulec, Donna Marino, Andrew O'Neill, Rob Poole, Brooke Rein, Benjamin Schmerler, Troy Segal, Robert Seixas, Yoji Yamaguchi and Sharon Yates.

The reviews published in this guide are based on public opinion surveys, with numerical ratings reflecting the average scores given by all survey participants who voted on each establishment and text based on direct quotes from, or fair paraphrasings of, participants' comments. Phone numbers, addresses, and other factual information were correct to the best of our knowledge when published in this guide; any subsequent changes may not be reflected.

© 2001 Zagat Survey, LLC
ISBN 1-57006-437-7

Contents

About This Survey 4
RESTAURANTS
  Map................................... 6
  Top Lists............................... 7
  Directory
    Addresses, Phones, Ratings & Reviews 11
  Indexes
    Cuisines 46
    Locations 50
    Special Features 53
NIGHTLIFE
  Map................................... 58
  Top Lists............................... 59
  Directory
    Addresses, Phones, Ratings & Reviews 61
  Indexes
    Categories 90
    Locations 92
    Special Features 94
SHOPPING
  Map................................... 102
  Top Lists............................... 103
  Directory
    Addresses, Phones, Ratings & Reviews 105
  Indexes
    Categories 124
    Locations 126
HOTELS
  Map................................... 130
  Directory
    Addresses, Phones, Ratings & Reviews 132
ATTRACTIONS
  Map................................... 136
  Directory 137
LOCATION INDEX....................... 145
ALPHABETICAL PAGE INDEX............. 151

About This Survey

This guide is like no other that we have ever published: It is an amalgam of four of our *Surveys,* covering restaurants, nightlife, shopping and hotels in Downtown Manhattan, south of Houston Street; in addition, we have included listings for major attractions.

Our reason for creating this guide is to bring business back to the parts of New York City most seriously affected by the September 11 attack. In the wake of that tragedy, these Lower Manhattan neighborhoods were cut off behind police lines and in many cases without telephones, power or delivery of goods.

Although our municipal leadership moved quickly to repair Lower Manhattan's infrastructure and transportation network, many of these local businesses reopened to find that customers were scarce. To begin with, the loss of the World Trade Center and the evacuation of the World Financial Center cost local businesses 80,000 of their regular clients. Moreover, the tourists who provide the lifeblood of Little Italy, Chinatown, SoHo, TriBeCa and the South Street Seaport were few and far between in late September.

Fortunately, a series of promotions have helped encourage the return of commerce. However, there is a long way to go before we reach pre–September 11 levels of activity. Realizing this, Zagat Survey and Verizon decided to produce this guide. It covers what we believe are the leading destinations in the area, but far from all of them – for example, clothing shops, antiques dealers and art galleries have not been surveyed by us and, accordingly, are not included here. Nonetheless, we believe that people who come Downtown to see the sights, browse, eat, drink or spend the night will inevitably discover these other neighborhood businesses. A few establishments had yet to reopen as this guide went to press, but we have listed them with a note that they are temporarily closed. We look forward to welcoming them back soon.

The main point is that everyone needs to support these local businesses. If we don't, it is quite possible that many will be lost – and with each one lost, the terrorists will have gained another terrible victory.

So, if you want to have a good time and simultaneously do a good deed, our message is simple: come on down!

New York, NY
December 3, 2001

Nina and Tim Zagat

Restaurants

Restaurant Map

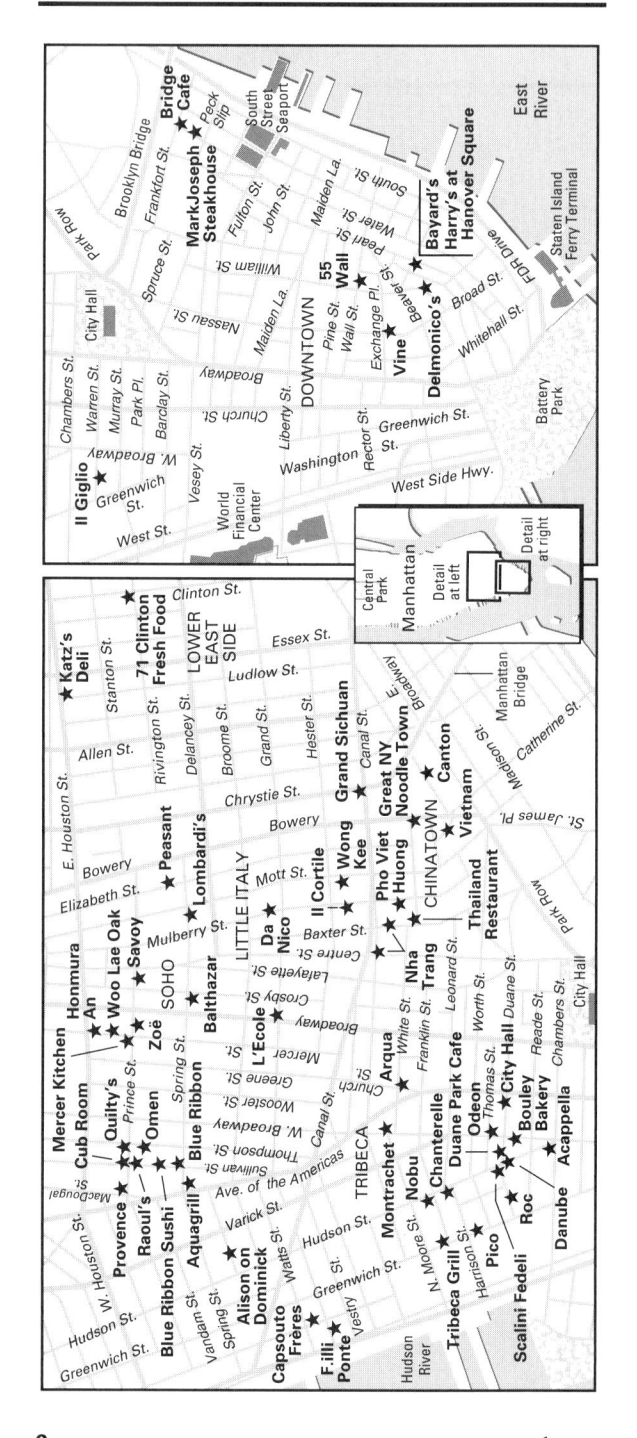

Top Rated Restaurants

Listed in order of Food rating

Top by Category

Food
- 28 Chanterelle
- Nobu
- 27 Bouley Bakery
- 71 Clinton Fresh Food
- 26 Montrachet
- Scalini Fedeli

Decor
- 28 Danube
- 27 Chanterelle
- 26 Hudson River Club
- 25 Scalini Fedeli
- Casa La Femme
- Nobu

Service
- 27 Chanterelle
- 26 Danube
- 25 Scalini Fedeli
- Nobu
- Montrachet
- Bouley Bakery

Late Dining
- 26 Blue Ribbon Sushi
- 25 Blue Ribbon
- 23 Balthazar
- Raoul's
- 22 Great NY Noodle Town
- 21 Bereket

Newcomers/Rated
- 25 MarkJoseph*
- 23 Wyanoka*
- Pico
- 21 Essex*
- 1492 Food*
- 20 Le Zinc

Newcomers/Unrated
- AKA Cafe
- Harrison, The
- Mooza
- Pfiff
- Sirocco
- 27 Sunrise Seafood

Old New York
- 1763 Fraunces Tavern
- 1794 Bridge Cafe
- 1875 Harry's/Hanover Sq.
- 1888 Katz's Deli
- 1890 Walker's
- 1891 Delmonico's

Quick Fixes
- 23 Snack*
- 22 Great NY Noodle Town
- Pepe Rosso
- 21 Bereket
- 20 Mangia
- Ferrara

Top by Neighborhood

Chinatown
- 25 Canton
- 23 Thailand Restaurant
- Nha Trang
- Grand Sichuan
- Wong Kee
- 22 Great NY Noodle Town

Financial District
- 24 Bayard's
- Roy's New York
- 23 Hudson River Club
- Vine
- 21 Cabana Nuevo Latino
- Bridge Cafe

Little Italy
- 24 Lombardi's
- 23 Il Palazzo*
- Il Cortile
- Nyonya
- 22 Peasant
- Pellegrino's

Lower East Side
- 27 71 Clinton Fresh Food
- 21 Katz's Deli
- Bereket
- 20 Oliva
- Torch
- Casa Mexicana

SoHo
- 26 Blue Ribbon Sushi
- 25 Aquagrill
- Honmura An
- Blue Ribbon
- 24 Omen
- L'Ecole

TriBeCa
- 28 Chanterelle
- Nobu
- 27 Bouley Bakery
- 26 Montrachet
- Scalini Fedeli
- Danube

---

* Low votes

www.zagat.com   7

Top by Cuisine

American
27 71 Clinton Fresh Food
25 Blue Ribbon
24 Bayard's
   Duane Park Cafe
23 Mercer Kitchen
   Vine

Chinese
25 Canton
23 Grand Sichuan
   Wong Kee
22 Great NY Noodle Town
   Peking Duck House
   Joe's Shanghai

French
28 Chanterelle
27 Bouley Bakery
26 Montrachet
24 L'Ecole
   Capsouto Frères
   Alison on Dominick

Italian
26 Scalini Fedeli
25 Il Giglio
24 Pepolino
23 Il Cortile
   Acappella
   Arqua

Japanese
28 Nobu
26 Blue Ribbon Sushi
25 Honmura An
24 Omen
21 Zutto
19 Obeca Li

Mediterranean/Spanish
23 Savoy
20 Oliva
   Mangia
   Flor de Sol
   Layla
18 Ñ

Noodle Shops
25 Honmura An
22 Great NY Noodle Town
   Pho Viet Huong
21 Big Wong
20 Bo-Ky
19 Pho Bang

Seafood
25 Aquagrill
24 Roy's NY
20 Le Pescadou
   Ping's Seafood
19 American Park
18 Lansky Lounge

Steakhouses
25 MarkJoseph*
22 Dylan Prime
20 Delmonico's
   Soho Steak
18 Lansky Lounge
   Harry's/Hanover Sq.

Vietnamese
23 Nha Trang
22 Vietnam
   Pho Viet Huong
21 New Pasteur
20 Bo-Ky
19 MeKong

Top by Special Feature

Brunch
26 Montrachet
25 Aquagrill
24 Capsouto Frères
22 Tribeca Grill
   Zoë
   Provence

Party Sites
23 Vine
22 Tribeca Grill
21 City Hall
20 55 Wall
19 Obeca Li
   Sammy's Roumanian

People-Watching
28 Nobu
26 Danube
23 Balthazar
   Mercer Kitchen
21 Cub Room
18 Canteen

Private Rooms
28 Nobu
27 Bouley Bakery
26 Montrachet
   Scalini Fedeli
   Danube
24 Bayard's

---

* Low votes

8   www.zagat.com

Under $40 Prix Fixe Menus*

Lunch

Arqua	20.00
Bouley Bakery	35.00
Capsuoto Frères	20.01
Chanterelle	20.01
Cub Room	20.01
Danube	21.00
Duane Park Cafe	20.01
Dylan Prime	20.01
F.ille Ponte	20.01
Gallery, The	20.01
Independent, The	19.95
L'Ecole	20.00
Le Zinc	20.01
Mercer Kitchen	20.00
Montrachet (Fri. only)	20.00
Nobu	20.00
Odeon	20.01
Quilty's	20.95
Tribeca Grill	20.00
Zoë	20.00

Dinner

Alison on Dominick**	30.01
Arqua	25.00
City Hall	30.01
Dylan Prime	30.01
F.illi Ponte	30.01
Gallery, The	30.01
L'Ecole	29.95
Le Zinc	30.01
Montrachet	36.00
Sal Anthony's S.P.Q.R.**	21.95
Screening Room**	35.00

---

* This list shows the lowest prix fixe menus available; there may be higher-priced options. Since prix fixe prices may change or be canceled at any time, check on them when reserving. Nearly all Indians serve an all-you-can-eat buffet lunch for $15 or less.

** Pre-theater only

www.zagat.com

Key to Ratings/Symbols

Name, Address & Phone Number

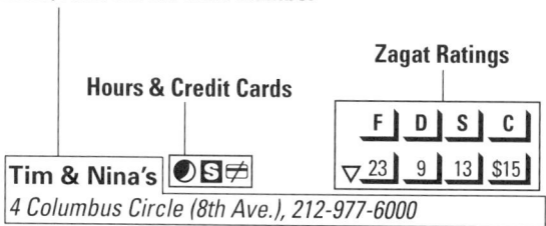

Hours & Credit Cards

Zagat Ratings

F	D	S	C
▽ 23	9	13	$15

Tim & Nina's ☾ S ⌿
4 Columbus Circle (8th Ave.), 212-977-6000

◩ Open 24/7, this "literal dive" is located in the IND station under Columbus Circle; as NY's first subway "soul pizza" stand, it offers "suckulent" slices with toppings of BBQ sauce, pork or fried chicken to harried strap-hangers "for little dough"; but for the "cost of your MetroCard" and the "need to shout your order" when the A train comes in, this would be "some trip."

Review, with surveyors' comments in quotes

Restaurants with the highest overall ratings and greatest popularity and importance are printed in CAPITAL LETTERS.

Before each review a symbol indicates whether responses were uniform ■ or mixed ◩.

Hours: ☾ serves after 11 PM
S open on Sunday

Credit Cards: ⌿ no credit cards accepted

Ratings: Food, Decor and Service are rated on a scale of **0** to **30**. The Cost (C) column reflects our surveyors' estimate of the price of dinner including one drink and tip.

F	Food	D	Decor	S	Service	C	Cost
23		9		13		$15	

0–9	poor to fair	20–25	very good to excellent
10–15	fair to good	26–30	extraordinary to perfection
16–19	good to very good	▽	low response/less reliable

For places listed without ratings or a cost estimate, such as an important **newcomer** or a popular **write-in,** the estimated cost is indicated by the following symbols.

| I | $15 and below | E | $31 to $50 |
| M | $16 to $30 | VE | $51 or more |

Restaurants | F | D | S | C |

Acappella | 23 | 21 | 23 | $57 |
1 Hudson St. (Chambers St.), 212-240-0163
■ Warblers have "something to sing about" at this TriBeCa Northern Italian renowned for its "over-the-top" service and high-"quality" meals polished off with "homemade grappa"; sure, you'll "feel like royalty", but be ready to "spend a bundle."

Ajisen Noodle S ⊅ | – | – | – | I |
14 Mott St. (bet. Chatham Sq. & Pell St.), 212-267-9680
A wall lined with bowls leaves little doubt about the concept at this new, inexpensive slurpeteria bringing Japanese flavor to the heart of Chinatown; expect a limited menu – several varieties of Ramen noodles, a number of small plates.

AKA Cafe ● | – | – | – | M |
49 Clinton St. (bet. Rivington & Stanton Sts.), 212-979-6096
This blithe Lower East Side American-Latino newcomer from the owners of 71 Clinton offers a quirky, midpriced tapas-style menu that includes seviche, empanadas and matzos in non-kosher oyster soup; its moodily lit mod interior makes even the nonhip feel hip.

Alison on Dominick Street S | 24 | 21 | 23 | $57 |
38 Dominick St. (bet. Hudson & Varick Sts.), 212-727-1188
■ "Harder to find than *Producers* tickets", this "heart-of-nowhere" SW SoHo Country French "labor of love" "hits the mark on all counts" with its "foodie heaven" cooking, "flawless service" and "less-is-more decor" that's so "romantic" it inspires "stolen kisses."

American Park at The Battery S | 19 | 23 | 18 | $48 |
Battery Park (opp. 17 State St.), 212-809-5508
◪ "Inspired views" of the "glorious harbor" and "Miss Liberty" "make up for any shortcomings" on the seafood-accented menu at this Battery Park American; sure, it's a bit "pricey" and "touristy", yet a "sorely needed" option for "amazing sunsets"; **N.B. closed at press time.**

Angelo's of Mulberry Street ● S | 20 | 14 | 17 | $38 |
146 Mulberry St. (bet. Grand & Hester Sts.), 212-966-1277
◪ This "Little Italy favorite" has been dishing out "big portions" of "zesty" Italian "red-sauce" fare for a century now and still enjoys a brisk trade of both natives and "throngs of tourists" despite "no decor to speak of" and "Grand Central"–like bustle.

AQUAGRILL S | 25 | 20 | 22 | $49 |
210 Spring St. (6th Ave.), 212-274-0505
■ "So many oysters, so little time" sigh "hooked" addicts in the "recurring crowd" at this SoHo "pearl" where "pristine seafood" served by "waiters who really know what they're talking about" delights deep-sea diners; no surprise, there are "people everywhere" "packed in like sardines" and you must "book way ahead."

---

www.zagat.com 11

Restaurants

| F | D | S | C |

Arqua ⑤
23 | 20 | 21 | $48
281 Church St. (White St.), 212-334-1888
■ When hankering for a "quick trip to Italy", nomads migrate to this "discreet little Northern Italian in TriBeCa" as much for its "generous portions of delicate cuisine" as for the way "they let you linger" in the "airy, welcoming room" straight out of a "Merchant Ivory movie."

Au Mandarin ⑤
20 | 17 | 18 | $32
World Financial Ctr., 200 Vesey St. (West St.), 212-385-0313
■ "You'll be in and out" of this WFC "chichi Chinese" "before you can finish reading your fortune cookie", which is fine with regulars who find "taking out better than eating in"; no wonder it's a "working lunch" "staple"; **N.B. closed at press time.**

Ba Ba Malaysian ●⑤⌀
▽ 21 | 15 | 14 | $20
53 Bayard St. (bet. Bowery & Mott St.), 212-766-1318
■ For a "delicious" meal "at the price of a martini Uptown", fans flock to this "heart-of-Chinatown Malaysian" that's "light on decor but heavy on flavor" ("the peanut pancakes will take you to heaven"); a "real sleeper", it works well whether on "jury duty" or "with a group."

Bacco ●⑤
▽ 20 | 18 | 19 | $42
150 Spring St. (bet. W. B'way & Wooster St.), 212-334-2338
◪ "Cozy" SoHo Italian offering "fresh, original entrees" and a stellar wine cellar that are both "nicely priced"; but dissenters say "early success went to their heads" and aren't sure they'll be back-o.

BALTHAZAR ●⑤
23 | 23 | 20 | $50
80 Spring St. (bet. B'way & Crosby St.), 212-965-1414
■ Keith McNally's "archetypal French brasserie" in SoHo is "as close to Paris as you can get" without paying airfare; "bustling, noisy and crowded", it's a "real happening" with "consistently good food" and "surprisingly good service", and rather than fight for a reservation at night, go for a more laid-back lunch or after 10 PM; if not everyone is a fan, they're a distinct minority.

Baluchi's ⑤
18 | 16 | 16 | $26
193 Spring St. (bet. Sullivan & Thompson Sts.), 212-226-2828
■ For a "little bit of Sixth Street" in SoHo, try this burgeoning Indian whose Italian-sounding "name makes no sense", yet it delivers "tastefully nuanced flavors" that are a "cut above" the rest.

Bar 89 ●⑤
16 | 22 | 15 | $28
89 Mercer St. (bet. Broome & Spring Sts.), 212-274-0989
■ "See-through bathrooms" with "glass doors that fog up when you close them" (make sure they're tightly shut) are conversation starters at this SoHo American that's more popular for its "fabulous" cocktails than for the "standard" bar chow and service.

Restaurants   F | D | S | C

Barolo ☻Ⓢ   19 | 21 | 17 | $49
398 W. Broadway (bet. Broome & Spring Sts.), 212-226-1102
◪ The very "Eden"-esque "garden is where it's at" say fans of this SoHo Northern Italian that might be on the "pricey" side but is "worth every penny" if you sit out back; but the "pretty food" and "pretty" patrons don't jibe with the "laughable" service out of a "Roberto Benigni farce."

Barrio ☻Ⓢ   ▽ 21 | 19 | 19 | $35
99 Stanton St. (bet. Ludlow & Orchard Sts.), 212-533-9212
■ Adding "even more creativity" to the "Lower East Side scene", this "minimalist" 24/7 Eclectic with a "funky vibe" turns out "dashing, modern dishes" in a "super-sketchy" nabe; though it's "way too loud", word is the chow is "much better than expected."

Bayard's   24 | 24 | 24 | $59
1 Hanover Sq. (bet. Pearl & Stone Sts.), 212-514-9454
■ "Like your rich uncle's club", this dinner-only Financial District French-American presents "civilized food in a civilized atmosphere" fitted out with a fine wine cellar as well as "relics of NY's maritime past"; though you'll contend with "bull-market prices", the payoffs are "dishes bursting with flavor", thanks to the "golden touch" of chef Eberhard Mueller (ex Lutèce, Le Bernardin).

Bereket ☻Ⓢ≠   21 | 7 | 14 | $14
187 E. Houston St. (Orchard St.), 212-475-7700
■ 24/7 Lower East Side über-"dive" offering "cheap Turkish" eats to "taxicab drivers" and "pub crawlers" who don't want the night to end; despite a "zero-decor" "cafeteria setting", it's "kebab heaven" for folks "on the run."

Big Wong Ⓢ≠   21 | 5 | 10 | $13
67 Mott St. (bet. Bayard & Canal Sts.), 212-964-0540
◪ Despite "cafeteria-like" looks and "surly" service, this Chinatown Cantonese noodle nook is "very popular" for "delicious" eats that you can cover "with the change in your pocket" – just "keep your eyes closed and your taste buds open."

Bistro Les Amis ☻Ⓢ   20 | 19 | 21 | $37
180 Spring St. (Thompson St.), 212-226-8645
■ "Sweet" SoHo bistro with a "convivial" "French feel" that draws passersby in to sample its "downright good" cooking; some propose "spiffing" things up, yet its overall "solid" performance is fine as is.

Bistrot Margot Ⓢ   19 | 16 | 17 | $31
26 Prince St. (bet. Elizabeth & Mott Sts.), 212-274-1027
■ Romantics seeking a "slice of French life" swoon over this modestly priced Little Italy bistro, even if others quip it's "just a very thin slice"; no question, the "quiet back garden" is a fine brunch getaway, particularly for puffers looking for a "Gauloises scene."

Restaurants

| F | D | S | C |

BLUE RIBBON ◑Ⓢ   25 | 18 | 21 | $47
97 Sullivan St. (bet. Prince & Spring Sts.), 212-274-0404
■ Whether you "go early" (to "get a seat") or "late" (to eyeball celeb chefs), there's "always a buzz" at this "trendy" Bromberg brothers SoHo Eclectic with a "cool crowd" and "scrumptious" menu; although they don't take reservations, the "good-looking" servers and "funny" barkeeps will "keep you amused while you wait."

BLUE RIBBON SUSHI ◑Ⓢ   26 | 18 | 20 | $47
119 Sullivan St. (bet. Prince & Spring Sts.), 212-343-0404
■ "Phenomenal", "magic-on-a-wooden-platter" sushi rivals the oh-so-"watchable" scene at this petite SoHo spot that's "hardly bigger than the cell phone they call you on when your table's ready" – but plan on "waiting a long time" to get in and "spending a lot" to get out.

Bo-Ky Ⓢ⌦   20 | 7 | 12 | $14
80 Bayard St. (bet. Mott & Mulberry Sts.), 212-406-2292
◪ "Affordable on a jury duty stipend", this Chinatown noodle shop is just right for "quick", "yummy" "one-bowl" meals that could "cure the common cold"; but the jurors' verdict on service and decor isn't so warm: "not the best."

Bot Ⓢ   ▽ 17 | 20 | 18 | $38
231 Mott St. (bet. Prince & Spring Sts.), 646-613-1312
◪ "Groovy mod" plastic decor is the conversation starter at this NoLita offshoot of Bottino, where hepcats tuck into "light, flavorful" Tuscan fare; though critics yawn "all style and no substance", those unwinding in its "awesome" garden are confident they'll "hammer out the kinks."

BOULEY BAKERY ◑Ⓢ   27 | 23 | 25 | $66
120 W. Broadway (Duane St.), 212-964-2525
■ For repasts that "transcend expectations", foodies cheer David Bouley's TriBeCa New French where "heaven on a plate" awaits either in its "relaxing", vaulted dining room or the "more casual" cafe, backed up by "polished", "not stuffy" service; **N.B. closed at press time,** the restaurant is currently serving the rescue workers at Ground Zero under contract to the Red Cross.

Bridge Cafe Ⓢ   21 | 18 | 19 | $41
279 Water St. (Dover St.), 212-227-3344
■ "If you can find it", this "real gem" under the Brooklyn Bridge puts out "consistently good" New American cooking in a brick-walled "old saloon" setting; though what's "cozy" for some is "cramped" for others, there's no question it's one of "NY's oldest" eateries.

Broome Street Bar ◑Ⓢ   16 | 14 | 15 | $23
363 W. Broadway (Broome St.), 212-925-2086
■ "Thank heaven" this "low-rent" SoHo beer-and-burger "joint is still jumping", supplying "adequate nutrition" in a "comfy old shoe atmosphere" at cheap tabs.

14   www.zagat.com

Restaurants   F | D | S | C

Bubby's 🆂   19 | 15 | 16 | $26
120 Hudson St. (N. Moore St.), 212-219-0666
◪ "Venerable" "TriBeCa original" that dishes out American "comfort food to the max" – including biscuits as "flaky" as its staff – and is noted for "celeb sightings"; those who can't handle the "weekend zoo" crowds say there are "better places to stargaze – like the planetarium."

Burritoville ◐🆂   16 | 8 | 12 | $12
144 Chambers St. (bet. W. B'way & Greenwich St.), 212-571-1144
36 Water St. (Broad St.), 212-747-1100
20 John St. (bet. B'way & Nassau St.), 212-766-2020
◪ For "cheap, addicting" fill-ups, this "omnipresent" Tex-Mex chain supplies "sombrero"-size burritos and "fire extinguisher"–worthy salsas; given the "ornery" service, "take it home or have it delivered."

Cabana Nuevo Latino 🆂   21 | 19 | 18 | $32
South Street Seaport, 89 South St., Pier 17, 3rd fl. (bet. Fulton & John Sts.), 212-406-1155
■ "Life's a party" at this "jumping" Cuban-Caribbean in the Financial District, where "delicioso" dishes, a "sexy" atmosphere and "rowdy crowds" add up to a "lotta bang for your pesos"; sun 'n' sea savvy surveyors dig its "sway-your-hips, gaze-at-ships" scene.

Cafe Colonial ◐🆂   20 | 20 | 17 | $40
276 Elizabeth St. (Houston St.), 212-274-0044
■ A "cool" colonial setting straight out of "Graham Greene" and "fine food" keep this "hip" Little Italy Brazilian-American hopping; diehards say they'd "like to be buried" with a dish of their "heavenly chocolate bread pudding."

Café Habana ◐🆂   20 | 14 | 15 | $23
17 Prince St. (Elizabeth St.), 212-625-2001
■ Following its appearance in a "Lenny Kravitz video", this Little Italy Cuban-Mexican has been "overrun with trendoids", who dig its "delicioso" chow; P.S. to beat the crowds, try the "take-out shop" around the corner.

Cafe Noir ◐🆂   17 | 18 | 14 | $32
32 Grand St. (Thompson St.), 212-431-7910
■ "Hipsters" "drink and nibble" on tapas and other "tasty" fare at this SoHo Med manned by an occasionally "surly" staff; to avoid the "dim" interior's "cigarette" haze, fresh-air fans "snag tables on the patio."

Canteen ◐🆂   18 | 21 | 16 | $42
142 Mercer St., downstairs (Prince St.), 212-431-7676
◪ Matthew Kenney's "retro-futuristic" SoHo New American is quite "a scene" where "beautiful" types nibble on "gourmet mac 'n' cheese" and other updated "comfort" classics while sitting on "fashion-forward orange chairs"; however, it won't be seen long unless he upgrades the "unfriendly" service and downgrades prices.

---

www.zagat.com   15

Restaurants | F | D | S | C |

CANTON ◐🅢⌿   25 | 14 | 21 | $43
45 Division St. (bet. Bowery & Market St.), 212-226-4441
■ NYers have been engaged in a "longtime love affair" with this "civilized" Chinatown Cantonese "classic", the *NYC Restaurant Survey*'s top-rated Chinese; don't bother "looking at the menu", just ask "charming" manager Eileen to guide you to the "superb" "seasonal specialties" that make meals here "worth the high cost" (for C-town).

CAPSOUTO FRÈRES 🅢   24 | 23 | 23 | $53
451 Washington St. (Watts St.), 212-966-4900
■ Your "taxi driver's nightmare" is finding this "out-of-the-way" ("Capsouto where?") TriBeCa "treasure" whose "imaginatively prepared" French meals, "romantic" setting and "welcoming" spirit merit a few "wrong turns"; luckily there are "no parking hassles", in case you drive yourself.

Casa La Femme ●◐🅢   17 | 25 | 17 | $54
150 Wooster St. (bet. Houston & Prince Sts.), 212-505-0005
▨ At this "transporting" SoHo "Arabian Nights" fantasy, "hookahs", "belly dancers" and "sexy" "private tent" Egyptian dining inspire "French kisses"; just don't let the "arrogant" staff and "large bill" break the "magical" mood.

Casa Mexicana ◐🅢   20 | 17 | 17 | $33
133 Ludlow St. (bet. Rivington & Stanton Sts.), 212-473-4100
■ A "genuine effort to upgrade" the "quality" of Lower East Side Mexican dining, this "lively" "surprise" specializes in "authentic" regional dishes and prices as well; most dub it a "classy" operation, though a few call it "over-yuppified."

Cendrillon 🅢   21 | 19 | 19 | $38
45 Mercer St. (bet. Broome & Grand Sts.), 212-343-9012
■ "Challenging but delicious" cuisine comes out of the SoHo kitchen of this "worldly" Filipino–Pan-Asian with a vaguely "French colonial" air; given the "warm hospitality", this "serene" spot is a "great de-stresser."

CHANTERELLE   28 | 27 | 27 | VE
2 Harrison St. (Hudson St.), 212-966-6960
■ "Beyond cloud nine and past seventh heaven" floats David and Karen Waltuck's TriBeCa French "classic that continues to impress" after more than two decades; sure, this "sustained champion's" cuisine is "sumptuous", though with a "beautifully appointed dining room" and "divine service", "it's about the total experience, not just one element"; "if you can afford it", it's "absolutely essential" for any serious food lover; dinner is $84, prix fixe only.

Chez Bernard 🅢   ▽ 19 | 17 | 18 | $41
323 W. Broadway (bet. Canal & Grand Sts.), 212-343-2583
■ With his "kisses good-bye", owner Bernard Eloy adds "an authentic touch" to his SoHo French bistro; the decor is a bit "dated", but the "food's tasty" and there's an added French accent – "smoking."

Restaurants | F | D | S | C |

City Hall | 21 | 22 | 21 | $49 |
131 Duane St. (bet. Church St. & W. B'way), 212-227-7777
■ The "City Hall you shouldn't fight", this "spacious, elegant" TriBeCa American brasserie hung with "wonderful photos of old NY" has "city politicians" and the "courthouse crowd" crowing over its "delicious" fare, overall "smooth operation" and ability to tax without complaint.

Clay ●S | ▽ 19 | 19 | 17 | $31 |
202 Mott St. (bet. Kenmare & Spring Sts.), 212-625-1105
■ It's "off-the-beaten-track", but Downtown types call this "hip" NoLita Korean as "good as its Koreatown" rivals; if the fare's only "quasi"-authentic, it's authentically cheap, and the "casual but chic" ambiance is genuinely a "scene."

Cosi ●S | 18 | 12 | 13 | $13 |
54 Pine St. (William St.), 212-809-2674
55 Broad St. (bet. Exchange Pl. & Beaver St.), 212-344-5000
■ Conspiracy theorists say "they must put something in the bread" at these sandwich shops "because it's amazing how the suits dive for the stuff when it comes out of the oven"; more and more NYers create lunches between their "addictive" slices.

Country Cafe S | 21 | 18 | 19 | $33 |
69 Thompson St. (bet. Broome & Spring Sts.), 212-966-5417
■ "Just plain adorable" SoHo bistro offering "delightful" Gallic fare with Moroccan "flair" in "minuscule" but "atmospheric" digs; though it's hard to "avoid the smoke", the "reasonable" prices are easier to take.

Cub Room ●S | 21 | 20 | 19 | $46 |
131 Sullivan St. (Prince St.), 212-677-4100
■ The "swinging bar" up-front contrasts with the "quiet dining room" in back at this SoHo New American where the "Frank Lloyd Wright"–esque decor is the "stunning backdrop" for "wonderful" cooking; the cafe adjunct serves "simpler, cheaper" fare.

Cupping Room Cafe ●S | 17 | 16 | 15 | $26 |
359 W. Broadway (bet. Broome & Grand Sts.), 212-925-2898
☒ Granted, it's "been the same for years", but this SoHo Eclectic is still dispensing "pretty good food" in a "tight", "living room–like" setting; the bohemian air extends to the "discombobulated" service.

Daily Soup ⊄ | 18 | 9 | 13 | $10 |
55 Broad St. (Beaver St.), 212-222-7687
☒ A "wide variety" of "homemade tastes" makes this Financial District cheap soup chain link "worthwhile" for "quick lunches"; still, some suggest that the "stainless steel" "assembly-line" ambiance and daily pricing mean "Campbell's need not worry."

www.zagat.com

Restaurants F | D | S | C

Da Nico ⑤ 21 | 16 | 19 | $33
164 Mulberry St. (bet. Broome & Grand Sts.), 212-343-1212
◪ "Old-fashioned" types, "tourists" and even "Rudy" sate their "Little Italy cravings" at this "charming" "Mulberry Street favorite" purveying "big portions" of "molto bene" "red-sauce" standards; "lovely" "garden seating" and "good value" add appeal, though a few skeptics shrug "hit-or-miss."

DANUBE ●◐⑤ 26 | 28 | 26 | $80
30 Hudson St. (bet. Duane & Reade Sts.), 212-791-3771
■ A Tyrolean "feather in the cap" for David Bouley, this "amazing" TriBeCa "dreamworld" transports diners with "heavenly, not heavy" Austrian cooking showcasing "spectacular" takes on schnitzel and other Viennese "classics"; set in a "gorgeous" "temple to Klimt" ("vat a room!") with "exemplary service" worthy of the "Hapsburg dynasty", it's way über the top but "hits every note" in Straussian style – "*ach, du liebe!*"

Delmonico's 20 | 21 | 20 | $52
56 Beaver St. (S. William St.), 212-509-1144
◪ The Street's "Gordon Gekko" stand-ins show up at this latter-day incarnation of the "historic" Financial District steakhouse where the "rich" woodwork, "staid service" and "perfectly charred" beef still "recall yesteryear"; though dismissed by some as "stodgy" and surviving "purely on its rep", all agree it works best "if it's on the firm."

Dim Sum Go Go ⑤ 19 | 13 | 15 | $23
5 E. Broadway (Chatham Sq.), 212-732-0797
◪ Run in part by epicure-on-the-go Colette Rossant, this newish Chatham Square dim sum parlor is an "instant favorite" among dollar-conscious dumpling devotees delighted with its "fresh", "artful" offerings and "innovative" "East-meets-West" approach (i.e. no carts); but a few take a dim view of service lapses and "garish decor."

Duane Park Cafe 24 | 20 | 22 | $49
157 Duane St. (bet. Hudson St. & W. B'way), 212-732-5555
■ Behind a "calm, quiet" exterior, this "unsung" TriBeCa New American squares off against its "flashier neighbors" with "delightful", "innovative" fare, a "refined" setting and "hospitality plus"; for "upscale" style at "downright reasonable" prices, alert types deem it a "real sleeper."

Dylan Prime 22 | 23 | 21 | $53
62 Laight St. (Greenwich St.), 212-334-4783
■ The times they are a-changin' at this TriBeCa outpost of "carnivorous pleasures", a "cool" "alternative" to the old "boys' club" "slab-of-meat" specialists; it offers "tasty" steaks, "oversized martinis" and "great sauces and sides" amid "sexy, dark" decor, which help compensate for a locale that's a ways "off the beaten trail."

18 www.zagat.com

Restaurants

| F | D | S | C |

Ecco
| 21 | 18 | 19 | $45 |

124 Chambers St. (bet. Church St. & W. B'way), 212-227-7074
■ "Unhip" it may be, but this TriBeCan satisfies its white-collar clientele with "superior" "old-world Italian food" served in an "elegant" barroom left over from the Gilded Age; regulars declare it a "real find" for "genuine" cooking, "comfortable surroundings" and "good service."

Edward's
| – | – | – | E |

136 W. Broadway (bet. Duane & Thomas Sts.), 212-233-6436
Formerly Bar Odeon, this new TriBeCa American bistro has hardly changed at all save for the name switch, with the softly lit space, low-key vibe and hip crowd all firmly in place; the kitchen staff has been retained too, so you can expect the same tasty vittles.

Eight Mile Creek S
| 21 | 16 | 20 | $46 |

240 Mulberry St. (bet. Prince & Spring Sts.), 212-431-4635
◪ An "unusual" "treat from Down Under", this surprisingly good Little Italy Australian lets "adventurers" "'ave some grilled" kangaroo or "amazing" emu carpaccio; despite a heartily "sociable staff", we hear gripes about "cramped space" and cramp-causing prices.

El Teddy's S
| 17 | 19 | 16 | $35 |

219 W. Broadway (bet. Franklin & White Sts.), 212-941-7071
◪ Still a "staple" in TriBeCa, this ultra-"funky" Mexican serves "fair" if "unamazing" food; the "fiesta" bar scene offers "killer margs" that "should be placed on the DEA's controlled substance list."

Essex Restaurant ●S
∇ | 21 | 19 | 20 | $40 |

120 Essex St. (Rivington St.), 212-533-9616
■ This upstart in the Lower East Side's Essex Street Market offers a midpriced melting pot of New American food enlivened by Jewish and Latin accents; though the room's "big", much of the limited, "creative" menu is of the small-plate variety.

Evergreen Shanghai ●S≠
| 18 | 12 | 16 | $26 |

63 Mott St. (bet. Bayard & Canal Sts.), 212-571-3339
■ Not your "run-of-the-mill Chinese", this basic C-towner pleases those who pine for "above-average", "genuine Shanghai" specialties and "attentive service"; greenhorns are intrigued by the "interesting" chow on the "cheap."

Excellent Dumpling House S≠
| 19 | 6 | 11 | $15 |

111 Lafayette St. (bet. Canal & Walker Sts.), 212-219-0212
■ Go back to "basics" at this Chinatown "dive" where there's "no decor whatsoever" to distract from the "mouthwatering" potstickers; it's a "must" for blowing a "jury duty" stipend, since it's really cheap and there's "no point in lingering."

www.zagat.com

Restaurants   F | D | S | C

Fanelli's Cafe ●S   15 | 15 | 14 | $23
94 Prince St. (Mercer St.), 212-226-9412

■ An "honest joint" that predates SoHo's "Prada mobs", this "gruff and lovable" 1872 saloon provides "well-priced" "bar food" in a "smoky", "checkered-tablecloth" setting; a "crowded", "convivial" "landmark" for beer, "burgers and bourbon", it's the "only plain eating" in the area.

Félix S   17 | 18 | 14 | $40
340 W. Broadway (Grand St.), 212-431-0021

◪ Thanks to a "smoke-blowing" "Euro" clientele and "snooty" service, this midpriced SoHo bistro is just the ticket for a bona fide Parisian experience; first-timers join the "lively" crowd for steak frites and other "solid", "simple" fare while trying to separate the "hip" from the "pretentious."

Ferrara S   20 | 14 | 14 | $17
195 Grand St. (bet. Mott & Mulberry Sts.), 212-226-6150

◪ Sure, it's "busy and touristy", but this circa 1892 "classic Italian patisserie" in Little Italy "keeps up the traditional quality" of its "delicious sweets" and coffees, and it's hard to refuse the "invitation to indulge" that cannoli craving.

55 Wall ●S   20 | 21 | 21 | $53
Regent Wall Street Hotel, 55 Wall St. (bet. Hanover & William Sts.), 212-699-5555

■ Its Wall Street site is a "virtue" for "impressing a client", and this "high-class" hotel New American follows through with "beautifully presented" food and "classic service"; insiders say this "power place" "deserves its reputation" for "civilized" dining and "insane prices" – "J.P." would approve.

F.illi Ponte   22 | 21 | 21 | $55
39 Desbrosses St. (West Side Hwy.), 212-226-4621

■ Get "away from everything" at this "beautiful", if pricey, TriBeCa Italian purveying "terrific", "hearty" food and a "spectacular view" of the Hudson; though it's now refurbished and living a "new life", traces of its former "*Sopranos*" days linger on.

Flor de Sol ●   20 | 22 | 19 | $38
361 Greenwich St. (bet. Franklin & Harrison Sts.), 212-334-6411

■ Let the "romantic" "good times" roll at this TriBeCa Spaniard where the "sexy scene" is easily as delightful as the "fab sangria" and "tasty" tapas; add "flattering" candlelight, "mysterious" "castle decor" and "dreamy" Don Juan waiters and it's no surprise surveyors shout "*olé.*"

1492 Food ●S   ▽ 21 | 20 | 21 | $36
60 Clinton St. (bet. Rivington & Stanton Sts.), 646-654-1114

■ This "welcoming" new Lower East Side Spaniard mixes "traditions", offering "good" Iberian fare jazzed up with "inventive" Mideastern flourishes; it's a way to explore multicultural possibilities over tapas and wine in a "warm", unpretentious setting.

Restaurants | F | D | S | C |

14 Wall Street Restaurant | 20 | 21 | 20 | $47 |
14 Wall St., 31st fl. (bet. Broad St. & B'way), 212-233-2780
◼ Once "J.P. Morgan's brownstone in the sky", this "elegant" Wall Street French aerie is still on the money with a "beautiful" "high-altitude" view, "discreet service" and "food worthy of a robber baron", but "a little expensive" if you're off the "corporate" tab.

Fraunces Tavern | – | – | – | M |
54 Pearl St. (Broad St.), 212-968-1776
21st-century patriots salute this recently reopened Financial District landmark that's been in business on and off for 239 years; although best known as the site of George Washington's 1783 farewell to his troops, today it welcomes diners with a reasonably priced, rejiggered menu of American classics served in a refurbished space that's worthy of flag-waving.

Funky Broome ●⑤ | 19 | 14 | 15 | $24 |
176 Mott St. (Broome St.), 212-941-8628
◼ "Change of pace" mavens turn to this Little Italy Chinese, a "modern" venue with "retro hip" neon lighting; its "huge menu" of "above-average" eats, at below-average tabs, offers a mix of "classics" and "interesting choices."

Gallery, The | – | – | – | E |
SoHo Grand Hotel, 310 W. Broadway, 2nd fl. (bet. Canal & Grand Sts.), 212-965-3588
The sunglasses-at-night crowd has a new destination at this reconceived, renamed American in the SoHo Grand (fka Canal House) that turns out three squares a day; expect a smallish, chic space that's somewhat more subdued than the neighboring Grand Bar, a hopping, DJ-equipped lounge that supplies the after-dinner entertainment.

Ghenet ⑤ | 20 | 15 | 18 | $25 |
284 Mulberry St. (bet. Houston & Prince Sts.), 212-343-1888
◼ Adventurers are "rewarded" with "succulent" specialties at this "easygoing" Little Italy Ethiopian where no-utensils dining makes for a hands-on "experience" using injera bread as a scoop spoon; with a "simple" setting and "sweet" staff, it's a "different" way to walk out "stuffed."

Gigino at Wagner Park ⑤ | ∇ 19 | 22 | 17 | $35 |
20 Battery Pl. (West St.), 212-528-2228
◼ Given the "million-dollar" harbor view, it's an effort to "notice the food" at this Battery Park City Italian; though the menu is less impressive than the original Gigino's, there's "more atmosphere" – after all, "sunset over the Statue is hard to beat"; **N.B. closed at press time.**

Gigino Trattoria ⑤ | 21 | 19 | 20 | $38 |
323 Greenwich St. (bet. Duane & Reade Sts.), 212-431-1112
◼ "Popular" with "neighborhood" types for its "homey atmosphere", this TriBeCa Tuscan is a "consistent"

www.zagat.com

Restaurants   F | D | S | C

performer with "simple yet noteworthy" food, "efficient service" and a "rustic", "barn-like" setting; all in all, a pleasant "peasant" night out.

Golden Unicorn 🆂   20 | 11 | 13 | $25
18 E. Broadway, 3rd fl. (Catherine St.), 212-941-0911
◼ At this Chinatown standout, the "superior dim sum" defines the "essence" of Hong Kong; despite "mayhem", "third-rate" service and a third-floor setting, you must expect "long weekend waits" for its "cheap", "classic" eats.

Good World Bar & Grill ●🅳🆂   ▽ 19 | 16 | 16 | $27
3 Orchard St. (bet. Canal & Division Sts.), 212-925-9975
◼ Sited far "off the beaten path", this easily affordable Lower East Side "hideout" offers "great-tasting plates" of "pure Swedish" food washed down by Scandinavian beer and cocktails; it's frequented by the "coolest hipsters", who mainly "go there to drink."

Goody's 🆂   20 | 8 | 14 | $20
1 E. Broadway (bet. Catherine & Oliver Sts.), 212-577-2922
◼ This "reliable" Chinatown Shanghainese boasts "rock-bottom prices" that make it easy to "indulge" in their "divine soup dumplings" and "heavenly" steamed buns; aesthetes insist the "tacky decor" matches the "tacky name."

Grace ●🅳🆂   18 | 18 | 17 | $33
114 Franklin St. (bet. Church St. & W. B'way), 212-343-4200
◼ Graced with a "big, long bar" and "wonderful woodwork", this modestly priced New American is a "sceney" spot to share "tasty" tapas-style dishes and sip "swell" cocktails with the "TriBeCa crowd"; adherents advise "go with a group" but "don't go hungry."

Grand Sichuan 🆂⇗   23 | 10 | 16 | $24
125 Canal St. (Bowery), 212-625-9212
◼ As "authentic as Szechuan can get" beyond the Chinese mainland, this C-towner lays out a "banquet" of "spicy, flavorful food" that's a perfect "escape from run-of-the-mill" dining; "cheap" tabs compensate for "hopeless decor."

Great NY Noodle Town ●🆂⇗   22 | 7 | 12 | $18
28½ Bowery (Bayard St.), 212-349-0923
◼ At this C-town noodle specialist, the "fabulous" chow and "late-late" hours make "real food" available even at 3 AM; sure, it's "unimpressive to look at", but the "authentic" fare and "dirt-cheap prices" more than compensate.

Grilled Cheese NYC 🆂⇗   ▽ 23 | 12 | 19 | $12
168 Ludlow St. (bet. Houston & Stanton Sts.), 212-982-6600
◼ You feel like a "kid" when clutching the "ultimate sandwich" at this Lower East Side storefront, which "upgrades" snacktime with a "fresh", "dee-lish" selection spotlighting its "melt-in-your-mouth" namesake; a "perky" staff and "happy wallet" pricing are bonuses.

Restaurants   F | D | S | C

Grill Room, The   ▽ 21 | 23 | 19 | $53
World Financial Ctr., 225 Liberty St. (West St.), 212-945-9400
◪ With a commanding view of the Hudson, this Financial District venue draws Wall Streeters for "pretty good", pretty pricey meat-and-potatoes American fare; though some say the service "falls short", it remains a "classy setting" for "entertaining new prospects"; **N.B. closed at press time.**

Hampton Chutney Co. ⑤   – | – | – | I
68 Prince St. (bet. B'way & Lafayette St.), 212-226-9996
Savory dosas are the specialty of this inexpensive, Indian-inflected SoHo American that's a clone of the popular Amagansett original; look for chutneys, of course, plus refreshing homemade drinks and some American-style sandwiches, all served at counters so slim you may want to opt for takeout.

Harbour Lights ●⑤   17 | 23 | 18 | $45
South Street Seaport, Pier 17, 3rd fl. (bet. Fulton & South Sts.), 212-227-2800
◪ The "lovely" harbor vistas and good bar make this "waterfront" South Street Seaport New American "not too shabby for a date"; however, some take a "dim" view of the "pricey", "passable", seafood-heavy menu; **N.B. closed at press time.**

Harrison, The   – | – | – | E
355 Greenwich St. (Harrison St.), 212-274-9310
From the owners of Chelsea's popular Red Cat comes this Med–New American that's the first eatery to open in TriBeCa since September 11th; like its sibling, it features inventive fare in cozy environs with an emphasis on hospitality, while downstairs a private dining room is in the works.

Harry's at Hanover Square   18 | 16 | 18 | $43
1 Hanover Sq. (bet. Pearl & Stone Sts.), 212-425-3412
◪ There's a "new" surf 'n' turf menu at this wood-paneled "Wall Street tradition" and though it may need to "work out the kinks", it's still "dependable" as an "all-guys" nexus made for "making deals" over "three-martini lunches"; for optimum enjoyment, use "someone else's credit card."

Herban Kitchen   20 | 15 | 17 | $28
290 Hudson St. (bet. Dominick & Spring Sts.), 212-627-2257
◪ "Cooking with a conscience" comes cheap at this SoHo organic American that leaves novices gasping "I can't believe it's tofu"; the "fresh, straightforward preparations" are polished by a "nice candlelit vibe" and "great garden", but tarnished by a "spacey staff that needs more protein in their diet."

HONMURA AN ⑤   25 | 24 | 23 | $49
170 Mercer St. (bet. Houston & Prince Sts.), 212-334-5253
■ For a "little Zen in SoHo", try this "soothing" Japanese that's as "elegantly understated as a pearl" and yields

Restaurants F | D | S | C

"brilliant" "hand-pulled soba noodles" in "Iron Chef–style" creations; it's "better than psychotherapy" (and about as "pricey") when you're dreaming about "true serenity in dining."

Houlihan's   11 | 11 | 12 | $25
196 Broadway (bet. Fulton & John Sts.), 212-240-1280
■ Perhaps "better in Indiana than NY", this Financial District burger-and-booze outpost is "adequate" for "office farewell luncheons", provided your coworkers can abide "mass-produced" grub "masquerading as food" served in "frat-boy settings."

HSF ●S⇌   19 | 12 | 13 | $26
46 Bowery (bet. Bayard & Canal Sts.), 212-374-1319
■ "Meals of many courses" are wheeled out at this Chinatown dim summer where there's a "large variety" of "tiny dishes" for patrons to "point" to; though the "recent renovations" are a "vast improvement", that "stadium fluorescent lighting" isn't.

Hudson River Club S   23 | 26 | 23 | $60
4 World Financial Ctr., 250 Vesey St. (West St.), 212-786-1500
■ "Keep an eye on your yacht" from windows overlooking the "captivating" harbor at this WFC American "class act" that works for both "power lunches" and "romantic" tête-à-têtes; "impressive" dishes inspired by the Hudson Valley and "attentive service" make the "memories linger", though your "platinum card" bill will jog your memory too; **N.B. closed at press time.**

Ideya ●S   ▽ 20 | 16 | 16 | $35
349 W. Broadway (bet. Broome & Grand Sts.), 212-625-1441
◪ Regulars "try not to get soused" too quickly and "miss the amazing food" at this "bustling", reasonably priced SoHo South American, but it's not easy given the "lively party atmosphere" and "potent" tropical drinks; "confused service" fits in with the overall "chaos."

Il Corallo Trattoria S   21 | 14 | 18 | $24
176 Prince St. (bet. Sullivan & Thompson Sts.), 212-941-7119
■ There could possibly be more kinds of "pastas than tables" at this "outstanding" Italian that's "sanely priced for trendy SoHo", so be "patient" when faced with "long waits" to get in.

Il Cortile ●S   23 | 21 | 20 | $45
125 Mulberry St. (bet. Canal & Hester Sts.), 212-226-6060
■ "Eating in the courtyard" Garden Room of this Little Italy Italian makes the "surprisingly good" fare "taste even more bella"; though prices may be "expensive for the area", a groundswell says it's the "best on Mulberry Street" – as well as the "prettiest."

www.zagat.com

Restaurants　　　　　　　　　　　F | D | S | C

Il Fornaio ◘　　　　　　　　　22 | 14 | 18 | $30
132A Mulberry St. (bet. Grand & Hester Sts.), 212-226-8306
■ Sample the "flavors of Little Italy" at this "homey" Italian that's "good for a quick bite" of "tasty" red-sauce fare; despite the "plain atmosphere", there are "nice-size portions for the price" and service is "superfriendly."

Il Giglio　　　　　　　　　　　25 | 20 | 23 | $59
81 Warren St. (bet. Greenwich St. & W. B'way), 212-571-5555
■ "Zesty food", a "great wine list" and "attentive service" keep this "expense-account" Italian almost as popular as its highly regarded cousin, Il Mulino, while its Financial District location works equally well for "jury duty" and "romantic dinners"; those who "wish it was open on weekends" will be cheered to learn that it has added Saturdays to its repertoire.

Il Palazzo ◘　　　　　　　▽ 23 | 19 | 21 | $38
151 Mulberry St. (bet. Grand & Hester Sts.), 212-343-7000
■ "Not touristy" Little Italy Italian known for "food that takes you to Rome" backed up by truly "friendly" service; besides, there's a "lovely outdoor garden", complete with "cute waterfall", so "for the price" it's hard to do better – just "leave room" for the "unbelievable desserts."

Independent, The ◐◘　　　　18 | 17 | 17 | $41
179 W. Broadway (bet. Leonard & Worth Sts.), 212-219-2010
◪ "Quintessentially TriBeCa" American duplex with a "quiet upstairs", "lively downstairs" and sidewalk cafe made for people-watching; some say it has "lost its spark", citing a kitchen that "needs to turn up the flavors a notch."

I Tre Merli ◐◘　　　　　　　17 | 18 | 15 | $42
463 W. Broadway (bet. Houston & Prince Sts.), 212-254-8699
◪ "You truly feel you're in SoHo" at this "fashionable" Northern Italian "scene" where you can "mingle with Euros" while nibbling on "ok pasta"; the "wine bottle–lined" digs and "models smoking cigars" provide distraction from the "aloof", "indifferent" waitrons.

Ivy's Bistro ◘　　　　　　▽ 21 | 16 | 18 | $37
385 Greenwich St. (N. Moore St.), 212-343-1139
■ For "mom's cooking away from home" in a "small" setting that has eluded TriBeCa's "attitude epidemic", this off-the-beaten-path Eclectic remains a "best-kept secret"; given the "reasonable" prices and "attentive" service, it's hard to understand why.

Jean Claude ◘⌀　　　　　　23 | 17 | 19 | $47
137 Sullivan St. (bet. Houston & Prince Sts.), 212-475-9232
◪ Infrequent fliers "save on airfare to France" and head to this SoHo "bargain" for a "near-perfect bistro experience"; despite sometimes "snobby" service and a crowd that "eats and smokes at the same time", the "absolutely delicious" cooking still "packs them in."

www.zagat.com

Restaurants | F | D | S | C |

Jerry's S — 17 | 14 | 15 | $29
101 Prince St. (bet. Greene & Mercer Sts.), 212-966-9464
◪ "Art world chic meets great french fries" at this "highbrow SoHo diner" popular for "simple, inexpensive" American grub; despite service that's "as variable as Bush's environmental policy", it's refreshingly "unpretentious."

Joe's Shanghai ●S⌀ — 22 | 9 | 13 | $23
9 Pell St. (bet. Bowery & Mott St.), 212-233-8888
◪ "Soup dumplings beyond compare" keep this C-town Chinese "famous", even if you must abide "rushed" service and "eating with strangers" at "communal tables."

Juniper Café ●S — ∇ 20 | 16 | 17 | $32
185 Duane St. (bet. Greenwich & Hudson Sts.), 212-965-1201
■ "TriBeCa's secret gem" may not be so secret anymore, since guests from nearby "boutique hotels have found it", but despite "vague" service, it still "charms" with "original" New American fare and a "mellow", "low-lit" setting.

Kam Chueh ●S⌀ — ∇ 24 | 8 | 16 | $25
40 Bowery (bet. Bayard & Canal Sts.), 212-791-6868
■ "Meet what you eat" at this Chinatown "temple of seafood" where the still-swimming fare goes "straight from the tanks" to the kitchen; the resulting "dynamite" dishes and low prices compensate for the "Vegas"-meets-"Asia" decor and crapshoot service.

Katz's Delicatessen S — 21 | 10 | 12 | $19
205 E. Houston St. (Ludlow St.), 212-254-2246
■ This vast Lower East Side "Jewish deli theme park" is a standard bearer for "sandwiches no human can get their mouth around" and still remembered for the "I'll-have-what-she's-having" scene in *When Harry Met Sally*; it's "not for the dainty", but the "drab" decor, "barking waiters" and sea-of-humanity crowd are all "part of the experience."

Kelley & Ping S — 18 | 16 | 14 | $24
127 Greene St. (bet. Houston & Prince Sts.), 212-228-1212
◪ "Trendy types" frequent this "quirky" SoHo noodle shop/tearoom/emporium for "inexpensive" Pan-Asian nibbles in a très "cool" setting that's one part "Shanghai movie set", one part "Asian bazaar" and one part lounge; but cynics nix "spotty service" and less-than-stellar eats.

Kin Khao ●S — 21 | 18 | 16 | $32
171 Spring St. (bet. Thompson St. & W. B'way), 212-966-3939
■ "Sticky rice" adherents tout the "terrific Thai" treats at this "trendy", tight SoHo scene frequented by a "too beautiful" "Downtown" crowd; to see in the "pitch-black" room, bring your "infrared glasses", and plan for a wait that's "longer than the meal itself."

Restaurants   F | D | S | C

Kitchen Club ⓢ   ▽ 22 | 19 | 21 | $44
30 Prince St. (Mott St.), 212-274-0025
■ Despite some "kooky combos", chef-owner Marja Samson's "inventive" NoLita Japanese-Eclectic generally serves "delicious" food with a "personal touch"; "say hello" to her dog (who will "visit your table"), and don't miss Chibi's, the adjacent sake bar.

Kitchenette ⓢ   20 | 11 | 13 | $19
80 W. Broadway (Warren St.), 212-267-6740
◪ "Fattening" "comfort food at its best" is served at this TriBeCa American that draws such "huge lines" for brunch that "by the time you get a table, it's time for dinner"; but fans downplay the service snafus and "cafeteria"-like digs, since tabs are dirt "cheap" and the eats darn "good."

Kori ⓢ   ▽ 19 | 19 | 19 | $33
253 Church St. (bet. Franklin & Leonard Sts.), 212-334-4598
■ "TriBeCa savvy meets Korean cuisine" at this "serene oasis" on a "bleak stretch of Church Street"; it "holds its own" with "creative creations" like the "super-value lunchboxes" served by a "friendly, discreet" staff.

La Mela ⓢ   19 | 12 | 17 | $34
167 Mulberry St. (bet. Broome & Grand Sts.), 212-431-9493
◪ "Little Italy meets *Animal House*" at this "rowdy", "off-the-wall" Italian where there's "no menu", meaning the "crazy waiters" will "just keep bringing you food" till you "explode"; though some revelers might find it "funny", it's not for "picky eaters", aesthetes ("do-it-yourself decor") or native NYers ("they treat everyone like tourists").

Lansky Lounge ⓢ   18 | 20 | 17 | $37
104 Norfolk St. (bet. Delancey & Rivington Sts.), 212-677-9489
■ They just "put up a sign", but you still feel "like a gangster or street urchin" slipping in through the "back-alley entrance" of this moderately tabbed Lower East Side surf 'n' turfer, which once housed a speakeasy and recently expanded by annexing most of the "old Ratners" space; night owls hoot it's a "better bar than grill."

Layla ⓢ   19 | 21 | 19 | $48
211 W. Broadway (Franklin St.), 212-431-0700
◪ "Glitz and shimmer" are the watchwords at this "over-the-top" TriBeCa Med-Mideastern from Drew Nieporent and Robert De Niro, where you can "channel Marrakech" while feasting on "unique", flavorful fare in colorful surroundings; still, some say it "lays la egg" and find the "pricey" "food secondary to the belly dancer"; **N.B. closed at press time.**

L'Ecole   24 | 19 | 22 | $42
French Culinary Institute, 462 Broadway (Grand St.), 212-219-3300
■ Graduate to dining cum laude at this SoHo FCI cooking school where promising pupils prepare pantastic food at

www.zagat.com   27

Restaurants | F | D | S | C |

"giveaway prices" ($29.95 five-course tasting menu); delighted "guinea pigs" declare "these students can practice on me anytime."

Le Gamin ●S≠ | 18 | 16 | 12 | $21 |
50 MacDougal St. (bet. Houston & Prince Sts.), 212-254-4678
◪ When "crêpe cravings" erupt, try this SoHo French cafe where the style is "Left Bank" and the mood is wired (thanks to the "rocket-fuel café au lait"); though it seems "you can sit forever" waiting for service, it eventually "comes with a cute accent."

Le Jardin Bistro S | 21 | 20 | 19 | $39 |
25 Cleveland Pl. (bet. Kenmare & Spring Sts.), 212-343-9599
■ In cool climes, this Little Italy French bistro evokes "lace-curtain Paris", while in warmer months the action moves to its "transporting garden" "roofed with so many grapevines" that it's "practically a vineyard"; year-round, there's "pleasant", "reliable" fare to be had at modest prices.

Le Pain Quotidien S≠ | 20 | 17 | 15 | $22 |
100 Grand St. (Mercer St.), 212-625-9009
■ "Quintessential" Belgian bakery/cafe in SoHo that draws "beautiful people with fat wallets" and a yen for "unbelievable bread and pastries"; lonely hearts say their "brilliant" "community tables" are "like having a meal at a Hamptons summer share."

Le Père Pinard ●S | ▽ 20 | 18 | 18 | $31 |
175 Ludlow St. (Houston St.), 212-777-4917
■ Say "*au revoir*" to NY and "*bonjour*" to France at this "cute" "Country French" bistro brimming with "young" Lower Eastsiders; everything's "authentic" here, including the "hearty, traditional" fare, "well-rounded wine list", "cramped", "smoky, noisy", "shabby-chic" interior and sometime "erratic service."

Le Pescadou ●S | 20 | 16 | 18 | $45 |
18 King St. (6th Ave.), 212-924-3434
◪ "You'll feel like family" (thanks to "congenial" host-owner Chuck) at this French seafooder serving "delish fish" in a bistro-style setting complete with "great outdoor seating" perfect for taking in the "lively" SoHo scene; penny-pinchers warn "Le Pesca-don't."

Le Zinc ●S | 20 | 18 | 20 | $40 |
139 Duane St. (bet. Church St. & W. B'way), 212-513-0001
◪ Chanterelle's new "casual" cousin has "hit the ground running" in TriBeCa with a roster of "superior" French "bistro comfort food" and a mostly "on-top-of-it" staff; though critics complain that it's "too loud" and "spare" ("great gallery posters" notwithstanding), it has been "a scene" from the get-go, particularly at the "beautiful", "crowded" zinc bar.

Restaurants   F | D | S | C

Lili's Noodle Shop & Grill S   18 | 15 | 16 | $22
102 North End Ave. (bet. Murray & Vesey Sts.), 212-786-1300
■ "Fun for a fast bite", this Battery Park City Chinese ladles out "wide choices" of "belly-filling soups" that amount to "bargains in a bowl"; given the "bright, cheerful" decor, slurpers say it's a "notch above" the typical noodle house; **N.B. closed at press time.**

Little Italy Pizza   20 | 8 | 14 | $10
182A Varick St. (bet. Charlton & King Sts.), 212-366-5566
11 Park Pl. (bet. B'way & Church St.), 212-227-7077
☑ "Authentic, basic slices" – "crust, sauce, cheese and grease" – make for a "cheap", "quick" meal at these decidedly "no-frills" pizzerias; they're "a mob scene at lunch", but the "endless lines" move fast thanks to "abrupt" but efficient service.

Lombardi's S⌀   24 | 12 | 15 | $21
32 Spring St. (bet. Mott & Mulberry Sts.), 212-941-7994
■ "The best pizzas in Manhattan" (and a "close second" to Brooklyn's Grimaldi's) emerge in Little Italy from this "unassuming", "historic" Italian's coal ovens, "crispy-crust" "beauties" that sustain fans through "daunting lines" and "tight quarters"; according to addicts, the trademark clam pie "will take your breath away."

L'Orange Bleue ●S   19 | 19 | 18 | $37
430 Broome St. (Crosby St.), 212-226-4999
■ A "lively SoHo scene" flourishes at this "exciting" French-Moroccan "surprise", where the "Euro"-heavy, French-speaking, Gauloise-smoking crowd likes to "let loose", particularly on Monday nights "with the belly dancer"; as for the "tasty" food, there's "something for everyone", and an equally "yummy" staff.

Lucky Strike ●S   16 | 16 | 15 | $31
59 Grand St. (bet. W. B'way & Wooster St.), 212-941-0479
■ "Still lit after all these years", this "reasonably priced" SoHo "classic" French bistro is noteworthy for its "late-night" hours; once trendy, these days it's more a "local" spot, which is fine with regulars who like its "killer" cocktails and "smoke-anywhere policy."

L'Ulivo Focacceria ●S⌀   – | – | – | M
184 Spring St. (Thompson St.), 212-343-1445
The laid-back ambiance at this SoHo Italian, especially in the sidewalk seating, makes diners feel like they're on the streets of Rome – though neither lira nor credit cards work here; the focaccia, pizza and other no-nonsense dishes come at very affordable prices.

Mandarin Court S   20 | 9 | 12 | $21
61 Mott St. (bet. Bayard & Canal Sts.), 212-608-3838
■ Dim sum devotees dive into the "delicious, diverse" selection of "tasty" "tidbits" at this "cheap", "reliable"

Restaurants   F D S C

Chinatown "standby"; it's "busy, loud" and "bland"-looking, with "smileless service", but those in-the-know "ignore the decor" and just "dig in."

Mangia   20 | 13 | 13 | $20
Trump Bldg., 40 Wall St. (bet. Broad & William Sts.), 212-425-4040

◪ This "crowded" Mediterranean "neo-cafeteria" elevates lowly lunch to a new level, thanks to a range of choices that makes customers feel "like kids in a candy store"; whether for eat in or take out, they "redefine fast food" for the better, while still keeping it affordable for the average salaried Joe and Jane.

Manhattan Bistro S   ▽ 19 | 18 | 17 | $39
129 Spring St. (bet. Greene & Wooster Sts.), 212-966-3459

◪ Steak frites the "Parisienne" way are the specialty of this "old-fashioned" French bistro that has managed to remain "low-key" and "not too trendy" despite its SoHo locale; though the blasé may find it "unremarkable", most sum it up in a word: "bon."

MarkJoseph Steakhouse   ▽ 25 | 22 | 26 | $55
261 Water St. (off Peck Slip), 212-277-0020

■ An "exceptional" "new steakhouse on this side of the Brooklyn Bridge", this highly rated Financial District chop shop draws ardent applause for being "more convenient and friendly than Luger's"; despite just-the-facts-ma'am decor and "not cheap" pricing, fans are convinced it "will become a staple."

Mary Ann's S⌀   17 | 13 | 15 | $24
107 W. Broadway (Reade St.), 212-766-0911

■ "Every day is Cinco de Mayo" at this "festive", "noisy" Tex-Mex in TriBeCa, where the "killer margs" and "tasty", "generous portions" at "peso prices" ensure there's always a "crowd."

MeKong Restaurant S   19 | 16 | 17 | $29
44 Prince St. (bet. Mott & Mulberry Sts.), 212-343-8169

■ "Post–gallery openings", this Little Italy Vietnamese fills the bill with "reliably tasty" edibles, low prices and a "hip", "fun Downtown feel" best appreciated in the "outdoor seats"; never mind if "the place needs a decorator", just focus on the "cool crowd."

Mercer Kitchen, The ●S   23 | 23 | 19 | $51
Mercer Hotel, 99 Prince St. (Mercer St.), 212-966-5454

◪ Fast becoming a "SoHo landmark", Jean-Georges Vongerichten's "ab fab" French–New American is "still a scene" supplying "star sightings galore" – even if the "sexy", "subterranean" setting is nearly "too dark to see" who's at the next table; though costly, the "creative" cuisine always "delivers", as does the "hip" staff that "doubles as eye candy" and attitude exemplars.

Restaurants

| F | D | S | C |

Mexican Radio ●S | 19 | 15 | 16 | $25 |
19 Cleveland Pl. (bet. Kenmare & Spring Sts.), 212-343-0140
◪ "Don't touch that dial": in its new NoLita digs, this "above-average Mexican" finally has some elbow room, although it may be too dark to see; while nostalgists miss the old "charm", "killer margaritas" and "tasty" "grub" "cut through any static."

Mezzogiorno ●S | 20 | 17 | 18 | $40 |
195 Spring St. (Sullivan St.), 212-334-2112
■ "When in SoHo, you can't go wrong" at this "little restaurant with the big brick oven", where the classic eats are "wonderful", the crowd's "young and fun" and the sidewalk tables are "outstanding for celeb sightings"; so what if the staff is "slightly condescending?" – the place "never disappoints."

MONTRACHET | 26 | 21 | 25 | $66 |
239 W. Broadway (bet. Walker & White Sts.), 212-219-2777
■ Ever a "model" for "gracious dining", this TriBeCa French "pioneer" is a "total pleasure" with "superior", "carefully orchestrated cuisine", a "terrific wine list" and "marvelous service"; the Friday $20 prix fixe lunch remains a "great deal", and despite hints that the "'80s" decor "needs sprucing up", most agree Drew Nieporent's beloved "baby never grows old."

Mooza ●S | – | – | – | M |
191 Orchard St. (bet. Houston & Stanton Sts.), 212-982-4770
Orchard Street continues to gentrify, as the adeptly prepared food at this new Mediterranean-Italian demonstrates; despite decor that madly mixes mosaic tile and leopard-skin prints, its prices satisfy Lower East Side budgets, while its garden is priceless.

Ñ ●S⊘ | 18 | 18 | 14 | $27 |
33 Crosby St. (bet. Broome & Grand Sts.), 212-219-8856
◪ "Cute as a button", "closet"-size SoHo tapas bar that's "packed all the time" with Downtowners grazing happily; if lack of space and "absent service" get you down, clearly you need another drink to make it all seem "sexy."

Namaskaar S | ∇ 22 | 17 | 20 | $29 |
337A W. Broadway (Grand St.), 212-625-1112
■ This SoHo Indian is a "find" for "thoughtfully prepared" fare "with just the right level of spice"; its "friendly staff" and "reasonable prices" are most "welcome" in this high-stepping locale, leading some to wonder "why it's so quiet."

Nam Phuong S | ∇ 20 | 11 | 16 | $22 |
19 Sixth Ave. (bet. Walker & White Sts.), 212-431-7715
■ TriBeCans tout the "healing soups" and other "fresh", "consistently good" dishes at this "authentic" Vietnamese; given the "sweet" staff and "cheap prices", any "fussing" over the plain decor "is not in order."

www.zagat.com

Restaurants F | D | S | C

Nello ◐ S 18 | 17 | 17 | $54
475 W. Broadway (Houston St.), 212-677-7172
◪ "Bring your shades", because this SoHo Northern Italian is "fabulous" for Eurocentric "people-watching and table-hopping"; there's also "good food", but critics carp it's "molto expensive", with limited service "if you're not a household name."

New Green Bo ◐ S ⊘ ▽ 22 | 7 | 14 | $17
66 Bayard St. (bet. Elizabeth & Mott Sts.), 212-625-2359
■ This "no-frills C-town haunt" may be "low on atmosphere, but what a selection" it's got of "tasty, cheap Shanghai" specialties (notably "mouthwatering" soup dumplings); many rate it "one of the best", hence it's usually "crowded."

New Pasteur S ⊘ 21 | 8 | 15 | $17
85 Baxter St. (bet. Bayard & Canal Sts.), 212-608-3656
■ A "jury-duty favorite", this "Chinatown staple" courts favor with "knockout" Vietnamese cuisine; the judicious judge it "hard on the eyes" but "easy on the taste buds" and "too cheap to be true."

Nha Trang S 23 | 8 | 15 | $18
87 Baxter St. (bet. Bayard & Canal Sts.), 212-233-5948 ⊘
148 Centre St. (bet. Walker & White Sts.), 212-941-9292
■ Despite the "cheesy decor", "dynamite Vietnamese" cooking, "great value" and "speedy service" make this "popular" C-towner the "best part of doing jury duty"; the newish Centre Street addition means "less crowding", though purists "prefer the original."

Nice Restaurant S 19 | 10 | 13 | $26
35 E. Broadway (bet. Catherine & Market Sts.), 212-406-9510
◪ Join the "banquet" at this Chinatown "extravaganza", a "noisy, auditorium-like" space where "crowds of locals" feast on "elaborate" Cantonese and dim sum; there's an "endless wait" and decor is "completely lacking", but for "top-tier" eating, the "name says it all."

NOBU S 28 | 25 | 25 | $70
105 Hudson St. (Franklin St.), 212-219-0500
■ It's next to impossible to get a seat (they don't always pick up the phone) at Nobu Matsuhisa's Japanese-Peruvian "classic" in TriBeCa, where the "incredible" offerings prove "some things are worth the wait"; expect "dining as theater" in a "richly atmospheric" setting "packed with celebs", but be prepared for "car payment"–worthy prices; P.S. those who "can't plan two months ahead" opt for Nobu's "gorgeous" Next Door sibling offering equally "brilliant food" for a "little less", without reservations.

Novecento ◐ S 19 | 17 | 16 | $38
343 W. Broadway (bet. Broome & Grand Sts.), 212-925-4706
◪ "Muy bueno" is the verdict on this SoHo Argentine "meat bar/restaurant" that may be "smoky", "chaotic"

Restaurants   F | D | S | C

and "beyond crowded", but makes for "sexy" "fun" thanks to its "oh-so-Euro" crowd and "feast-your-eyes staff."

Nyonya ◐S⌿   23 | 14 | 15 | $21
194 Grand St. (bet. Mott & Mulberry Sts.), 212-334-3669
◪ "You can't go wrong" at this bargain Little Italy Malaysian, since everything's "exotic" and "delicious" as well as "hot and spicy"; forget the "forgettable decor", "so-so service" and "long lines" – the incredibly "cheap" bills make it all worthwhile.

Obeca Li   19 | 22 | 17 | $44
62 Thomas St. (bet. Church St. & W. B'way), 212-393-9887
◪ Even though the Pan-Asian food's quite good, it is outshined by the "really modern" look of this "multi-level" TriBeCan; however, many appear to think that the "MIA" service is "just ridiculous."

Odeon ◐S   19 | 18 | 18 | $41
145 W. Broadway (bet. Duane & Thomas Sts.), 212-233-0507
■ "In a class all its own", this TriBeCa "legend" remains "forever hip" and "still relevant" thanks to enduring "good karma" matched by "steady" American-French fare; it's "at its best" "late night", when the "glorified" "diner decor" "looks better" – especially after the "celebs" and "arty" folk toddle in.

Oliva ◐S   20 | 15 | 17 | $36
161 E. Houston St. (Allen St.), 212-228-4143
■ "Innovative" "modern Basque" cookery combines with a "cool, buzzing vibe" to make this Lower East Side "hole-in-the-wall" quite the "hip haven"; loyal subjects say "tapas reign", but the "high-volume", "energetic" "party scene" may dethrone it.

Omen ◐S   24 | 20 | 21 | $48
113 Thompson St. (bet. Prince & Spring Sts.), 212-925-8923
■ For two decades, this SoHo Japanese has been among the "truest" of the genre, serving "delectable" "Kyoto-style" fare that many consider sheer "perfection"; "respectful service" and a "tranquil" setting reinforce the "meditative" mood that is likely to continue after you pay the bill.

Once Upon a Tart S   20 | 13 | 13 | $16
135 Sullivan St. (bet. Houston & Prince Sts.), 212-387-8869
◪ "Heavenly buttermilk scones" in the AM, "creative gourmet sandwiches" for lunch and "scrumptious" "sweet treats" all day long keep this "tiny", "no-glamour" SoHo cafe "busy"; the "aloof staff" also provides a "complimentary inferiority complex with every muffin."

Onieal's Grand St. ◐S   ∇ 18 | 22 | 20 | $41
174 Grand St. (bet. Centre & Mulberry Sts.), 212-941-9119
■ "Elegance without pretension" is the hallmark of this "undiscovered" Little Italy New American in a "landmark

Restaurants F | D | S | C

building" that's awash in dark wood and "romantic lighting"; "delicious food" and a "comfy bar" make it a more than "pleasant find."

Oriental Garden ●⑤ ▽ 24 | 11 | 16 | $32
14 Elizabeth St. (bet. Bayard & Canal Sts.), 212-619-0085
■ "If it swims, they've got it" could be the motto of this all-white, fish tank–lined, Hong Kong–style seafood house in Chinatown; though usually crowded with C-town types, given the "excellent" quality and modest prices of its cuisine, it's surprising that so few of our seafood-savvy surveyors seem to have tried it.

Oro Blu ▽ 20 | 18 | 20 | $39
333 Hudson St. (Charlton St.), 212-645-8004
■ A "standout" in the West SoHo "dining wasteland", this "open, airy" Italian is "lively" at lunch with neighboring "ad and printing" folk who praise its "above-average" food, "personable" service and "good food-to-dollar ratio."

Paladar ⑤∅ ▽ 20 | 18 | 20 | $31
161 Ludlow St. (bet. Houston & Stanton Sts.), 212-473-3535
■ "Funky", wide-ranging Lower East Side Latino newcomer featuring "reliable Cuban dishes" accompanied by mojitos, caipirinhas and the like; the "cool" ambiance attracts correspondingly cool customers who dig the "cheap" tabs.

Pão! ⑤ 22 | 16 | 20 | $37
322 Spring St. (Greenwich St.), 212-334-5464
■ This "fun" Portuguese "haunt" parked in an "out-of-the-way" West SoHo nook has a "dark", "tight setting" counterbalanced by a menu of "bright, focused flavors"; loyalists tout its "authentic" atmosphere ("everybody smokes") and "inexpensive" tabs.

Peasant ●⑤ 22 | 20 | 19 | $47
194 Elizabeth St. (bet. Prince & Spring Sts.), 212-965-9511
■ "Cool" NoLita open-kitchen Italian with "fabulous", "simple cooking" from its "wood-burning" oven; if there's "nothing peasant-like about the prices" and its "limited" menu could use "subtitles", they've managed to "control the noise level" without dampening its "fun", "friendly" feel.

Peking Duck House ⑤ 22 | 14 | 16 | $32
28 Mott St. (bet. Chatham Sq. & Pell St.), 212-227-1810
◪ The "other dishes pale in comparison" to the "amazing" Peking duck at this Chinatown "classic" that's relocated and upgraded to mixed notices: new fans offer "kudos" to its "minimalist", "soothing" redo, but ex-fans "miss" its former "run-down" digs.

Pellegrino's ⑤ 22 | 17 | 20 | $38
138 Mulberry St. (bet. Grand & Hester Sts.), 212-226-3177
■ This "front-runner" stays a nose ahead of the Mulberry Street pack by serving "tasty", "fairly priced" pastas; though

Restaurants F D S C

you can expect the "same old" "tacky" Little Italy decor, service is "friendly" and it's "not overloaded with tourists."

Penang ●◐S   19 | 17 | 16 | $29
109 Spring St. (bet. Greene & Mercer Sts.), 212-274-8883
■ This minimally priced, "marvelous Malaysian" "mainstay" in SoHo comes with "thatch-roofed", "bamboo-riot" decor and a "sarong"-wearing staff; some dub the grub "uneven" and "wish the noise level was lower", but you don't get this "packed" without being very popular.

Pepe Rosso S⊘   22 | 11 | 14 | $17
149 Sullivan St. (bet. Houston & Prince Sts.), 212-677-4555
■ "Soul-satisfying" SoHo Italian that dishes out "cheap, tasty", "no-frills" fare in a "zero atmosphere" setting; to avoid the "brusque service" and get "paesano treatment", "order in Italian."

Pepolino S   24 | 18 | 23 | $42
281 W. Broadway (bet. Canal & Lispenard Sts.), 212-966-9983
■ "Tuscany" comes to TriBeCa at this "terrific" trattoria that's relatively "unfound" despite the "consistency" of its "simple" yet "inventive" menu, and even better, there's "no pretense" at this "family-run spot."

Petite Abeille S   19 | 13 | 16 | $22
134 W. Broadway (Duane St.), 212-791-1360
■ Those craving a "fix" of "Brussels"-style "comfort food" make a beeline for this "bargain" "Tintin-themed" TriBeCa Belgian; service can be "slapdash", but their "rickety wooden tables" are always "packed."

Pfiff ◐   – | – | – | M
35 Grand St. (Thompson St.), 212-334-6841
Set on a less-traveled corner of SoHo, this New American exudes a quiet-yet-cool vibe maximized by Orange Crush–colored banquettes and a compact bar made for sipping sexy cocktails; seafood with tropical overtones stars on its stylish midpriced menu.

Pho Bang S   19 | 7 | 12 | $16
6 Chatham Sq. (Mott St.), 212-587-0870
157 Mott St. (bet. Broome & Grand Sts.), 212-966-3797 ⊘
3 Pike St. (bet. Canal & Division Sts.), 212-233-3947 ⊘
■ "Great to duck into" for a "fast" slurp, this "no-decor" Vietnamese noodle chain ladles out "big bowls of satisfying soup" at "lotsa locations" in Chinatown; plentiful portions and "dirt-cheap" prices add up to the best "bang pho the buck" going.

Pho Viet Huong S   22 | 10 | 16 | $19
73 Mulberry St. (bet. Bayard & Canal Sts.), 212-233-8988
■ "You get more than you pay for" at this "supercheap" Chinatown Vietnamese maker of "marvelous noodle soups"

www.zagat.com   35

Restaurants F | D | S | C

cataloged on a menu that seems to "extend forever"; it may be "plain", but it's "clean and neat", and "perfect for those jury-duty lunches."

Pico S 23 | 22 | 21 | $61
349 Greenwich St. (bet. Harrison & Jay Sts.), 212-343-0700
◪ Ex JUdson Grill chef John Villa's "glorious" "take on" Portuguese cuisine at this TriBeCa "newcomer" has made it a fast "favorite" of foodies, while its "chic" space has set "romantics" swooning; if a "disappointed" few deem it "overhyped" and rather "overpriced", that's no surprise when expectations have been set so high.

Ping's Seafood ●S 20 | 11 | 13 | $30
20 E. Broadway (bet. Catherine & Market Sts.), 212-965-0808
22 Mott St. (bet. Bayard & Pell Sts.), 212-602-9988
■ "Some of the freshest, subtlest food" in town can be had at this "Hong Kong–style" duo where the "exotic" seafood is "plucked from the tanks" and "artfully" prepared by "cooks who speak fluent delicious" – even if the servers suffer from "language barriers."

Pizzeria Uno Chicago ●S 15 | 12 | 13 | $20
South Street Seaport, 89 South St. (Pier 17), 212-791-7999
◪ It's "not gourmet", but this Financial District pizzeria is a "reliable standby" for "moms with kids" and others looking for "cheap" "group binges" on "huge" deep-dish pies sliced up in "laid-back", "bar-like" environs; skeptics scoff it's barely a "step above fast food."

Positano Ristorante ●S ▽ 20 | 16 | 18 | $35
122 Mulberry St. (bet. Canal & Hester Sts.), 212-334-9808
■ "A cut above" the "typical turista" joints in Little Italy, this "old-school" Italian is reliable for "reasonably priced", "homey" pastas and other classics in "generous portions"; service is "attentive", but the "rustic" interior is nothing to write home about.

Provence ●S 22 | 22 | 20 | $51
38 MacDougal St. (Prince St.), 212-475-7500
■ "Even in winter", this "romantic" SoHo bistro "transports" diners to sunnier climes with its "delightful" Provençal fare and "picturesque" interior with "windows for dreamers" up-front, "gorgeous flowers" everywhere and a "pretty" back garden "for kissing over moules"; "knowledgeable, friendly" service is icing on the cake.

Quartino S ▽ 19 | 18 | 18 | $34
21 Peck Slip (Water St.), 212-349-4433
■ Modestly priced, "up-and-coming" South Street Seaport Northern Italian that's following an unusual approach: its "small menu" of "delicious" dishes is limited to light, heart-"healthy" choices (nothing fried or even sautéed), accompanied by "good wines" and served in "cute quartinos"; locals "hope the tourists don't discover it."

Restaurants   F | D | S | C

Raoul's ◐ S   23 | 20 | 19 | $49
180 Prince St. (bet. Sullivan & Thompson Sts.), 212-966-3518
■ "Perfect for a late-night rendezvous" and for "footsie under the table", this "timeless" SoHo French bistro is hard to beat; besides a "sultry, sexy" vibe, it offers "quality" cooking, especially the "must-have steak au poivre"; if you can arrange it, "sit outside on the patio."

Ratner's S   16 | 10 | 13 | $25
138 Delancey St. (bet. Norfolk & Suffolk Sts.), 212-677-5588
◪ "Not what it used to be", this longtime Lower East Side "dairy queen" is now "much smaller" and no longer strictly kosher, inspiring a chorus of "oy veys"; though the "great blintzes" and rude waiters remain, many say the redo "killed the character"; N.B. open only Sundays, from 8 AM–8 PM.

Rialto ◐ S   19 | 20 | 18 | $37
265 Elizabeth St. (bet. Houston & Prince Sts.), 212-334-7900
◪ Cushy "red leather booths", "warm lighting" and a "romantic garden" make this "sexy" Little Italy American very "hot date"–worthy, with food that's "pretty good" but really beside the point; still, the price is right and the "staff not nearly as pretentious as it could be."

Rice ◐ S ⇌   19 | 14 | 14 | $18
227 Mott St. (bet. Prince & Spring Sts.), 212-226-5775
■ Hipsters head for this "teeny" NoLita Eclectic for "clever", "healthy" meals based around "just what the name says"; sure, it's "cramped", "dark" and "cash-only", but it's so "cheap" you could "recycle some cans" to pay the bill.

Roc ◐ S   ▽ 23 | 22 | 21 | $50
190A Duane St. (Greenwich St.), 212-625-3333
■ "Big spenders, celebs" and "neighborhood" folk rub shoulders at this "hip" TriBeCa Italian "rookie" offering "fresh", "honest" cooking that's as "solid" as a you-know-what; even skeptics who find it "noisy" and "overpriced" admit the service makes you feel like part of "la famiglia."

Roy's New York S   24 | 20 | 21 | $51
Marriott Financial Ctr., 130 Washington St. (bet. Albany & Carlisle Sts.), 212-266-6262
■ "Paradise" comes to Lower Manhattan at this "original", if expensive, Asian seafooder from star Honolulu chef Roy Yamaguchi; expect an "innovative" use of "exotic flavors" and "airy" digs that feel almost "as laid-back as Hawaii"; **N.B. closed at press time.**

Salaam Bombay S   21 | 18 | 18 | $35
317 Greenwich St. (bet. Duane & Reade Sts.), 212-226-9400
■ "Indian food done right" lures locals to this "terrific" TriBeCa "standby" where the "spicy" food comes accompanied by "live weekend sitar music"; the AYCE $12.95 lunch/brunch is not only an "impressive" spread, but a "bargain" too.

---
www.zagat.com

Restaurants F | D | S | C

Sal Anthony's S.P.Q.R. S 18 | 18 | 18 | $37
133 Mulberry St. (bet. Grand & Hester Sts.), 212-925-3120
◪ "Reliable" platefuls of "heavy-on-the-sauce" Italian fare and a sprawling setting keep this Little Italy vet popular with "large parties" requiring "lots of space"; sure, it can be "loud" and "touristy", but the cash-strapped claim the prix fixe makes it all "worth it."

Sammy's Roumanian S 19 | 10 | 16 | $47
157 Chrystie St. (Delancey St.), 212-673-0330
◪ This "unique" "museum of Jewish eating" is "worth the schlep" to the Lower East Side for its "enormous", "clog-the-arteries" servings of mittel-Europa classics; one part rowdy "celebration", one part "nostalgia trip", it boasts a colorful staff and colorless "basement decor" – in sum, "go for the experience, stay for the heartburn."

Savore ●◐ S ▽ 21 | 18 | 20 | $43
200 Spring St. (Sullivan St.), 212-431-1212
■ SoHo's old guard "savors" this "traditional" "taste of Tuscany" where the "well-prepared" cooking comes in "comfortable" digs; it's also "affordable for the regular" diner – a "nice surprise" in this upmarket turf.

Savoy S 23 | 22 | 22 | $51
70 Prince St. (Crosby St.), 212-219-8570
■ "Romance personified", this SoHo Mediterranean presents "inventive", "beautifully thought-out" dishes in a "tasteful" duplex setting; though "pricey" (and prix fixe only upstairs), it's a "memorable" "date place" where "special occasions" are "really special."

SCALINI FEDELI 26 | 25 | 25 | $71
165 Duane St. (bet. Greenwich & Hudson Sts.), 212-528-0400
■ A "bright star" transplanted from the Garden State, this "classic Italian" gives TriBeCa a taste of "what dining's all about" via Michael Cetrulo's "impeccably executed" cuisine; despite the "very expensive" price tag, the "gorgeous", "quietly elegant" room (that once housed Bouley) and always-"gracious" service cause customers to count this "masterpiece" among "NY's finest."

Screening Room S 20 | 19 | 19 | $38
54 Varick St. (Laight St.), 212-334-2100
■ "Dinner and a movie" is the "concept" at this "hip" TriBeCa New American–cum–screening room that earns "two thumbs up" for providing a first-rate "date idea" and an "inventive menu" that's "better than it needs to be"; have a drink in the "cozy lounge" for a "fun" triple feature.

71 CLINTON FRESH FOOD S 27 | 17 | 22 | $53
71 Clinton St. (bet. Rivington & Stanton Sts.), 212-614-6960
■ All-out "enthusiasm" reigns at this "ultra-hip" Lower East Side storefront where chef Wylie Dufresne's "vibrant kitchen" is "hot" to the melting point, turning out "highly

Restaurants F D S C

imaginative" New American fare that elicits "wows"; despite "high-end" pricing, the "close" quarters and "star status" guarantee it's a "struggle to get in", at least until Dufresne moves to his new nearby restaurant, scheduled to open in the spring.

Shanghai Cuisine S ▽ 21 | 14 | 16 | $23
89 Bayard St. (Mulberry St.), 212-732-8988
■ "Soup dumplings are a must" at this "step up from the typical Chinatown joint", offering "very authentic", very low-cost cooking; no wonder its "1930s Chiang Kai-shek"–style room is "always crowded" – despite Mao-style service.

Sirocco ●S – | – | – | M
199 Prince St. (bet. MacDougal & Sullivan Sts.), 212-254-4040
This SoHo Mediterranean newcomer offers a midpriced menu by ex Calle Ocho chef Alex Garcia as well as an extensive tapas selection available till 2 AM; tasting-menu samplers, a sidewalk cafe and two *intime* balcony tables make this look like an instant winner.

Snack S ▽ 23 | 14 | 18 | $18
105 Thompson St. (bet. Prince & Spring Sts.), 212-925-1040
■ Once a snack bar and still "cozy", this "unpretentious" SoHo Hellenic demonstrates how "delicious" (and inexpensive) "homemade" Greek dishes can be; despite the name, everyone "leaves full", and it's already so "cramped" (12 seats) that fans "hope more people don't discover it."

Soho Steak S 20 | 16 | 17 | $38
90 Thompson St. (bet. Prince & Spring Sts.), 212-226-0602
◪ Contented carnivores continually claim this "cheap, cheerful" "crowded" SoHo French-American bistro is a "fabulous deal" for "no-frills" steak frites; though the "close" quarters draw brickbats, they can be a "plus" for "getting to know" the "trendy, pretty" folks at the surrounding tables.

Sosa Borella S ▽ 20 | 17 | 19 | $32
460 Greenwich St. (bet. Desbrosses & Watts Sts.), 212-431-5093
■ Operating out of a "quiet" corner of TriBeCa, this "affordable" Italian-Argentine "find" works as an "unusual" lunch locus for "robust", "finger-licking" sandwiches or as an "undiscovered" dinner destination for "grilled meats"; either way, the "warm" staff keeps things "casual."

Spring Street Natural ●S 19 | 17 | 17 | $26
62 Spring St. (Lafayette St.), 212-966-0290
■ This SoHo health food "tradition" keeps on "doing what comes naturally" with its "hearty" helpings of good organic grub (plus fish and fowl); despite an "amnesiac" staff, it's memorable as a "spacious", "cheap" alternative not limited to "seeds and weeds."

www.zagat.com

Restaurants   F | D | S | C

Starbucks   14 | 12 | 12 | $10
150 Varick St. (Spring St.), 646-230-9816 S
78 Spring St. (Crosby St.), 212-219-2961 S
125 Chambers St. (W. Broadway), 212-791-6368 S
291 Broadway (Reade St.), 212-406-5310 S
38 Park Row (Beekman St.), 212-587-8400 S
100 William St. (bet. John & Platt St.), 212-509-9709
45 Wall St. (bet. Pearl & William St.), 212-269-8717 S
100 Wall St. (bet. Front & Water Sts.), 212-809-1556 S
3 New York Plaza (at Water & Whitehall Sts.), 212-785-1082
55 Broad St. (Beaver St.), 212-742-2488 S
Plus other locations throughout the Downtown area
◪ Most "grudgingly" admit this "planetary ruler" brews up "damn good" "high-octane" java; even if boycotters berate the "bitter" brew as "totally overpriced", fans say "thanks a latte" for the "extra living room" – and easy access to Krispy Kremes.

Stella S   – | – | – | M
58 MacDougal St. (bet. Houston & Prince Sts.), 212-674-4968
A charmer that makes everyone feel like a regular, this SoHo newcomer serves satisfying New American fare with a slight Gallic accent; the menu flirts with the unexpected (rosemary ice cream cone, anyone?), while raw brick walls, cozy window seats and rustic wooden tables make for an inviting setting.

St. Maggie's Cafe   18 | 18 | 18 | $36
120 Wall St. (bet. Front & South Sts.), 212-943-9050
■ "Formal" Victorian decor and "reliable", if rather "run-of-the-mill", cooking make this Financial District American a "lunch mecca" and standby for "business occasions"; most agree its location closes the deal, given the "limited Downtown eating options."

Sweet-n-Tart ◐ S ⌀   20 | 10 | 13 | $18
76 Mott St. (Canal St.), 212-334-8088
20 Mott St. (bet. Chatham Sq. & Pell St.), 212-964-0380
■ A "massive menu" of Chinese "snack foods" allows you to mix 'n' match at these "cheap, fast" Hong Kong–style venues where the "unique" dim sum and tong shui (sweet soups "for what ails you") distract from the "tacky" surroundings; N.B. at the multi-level 20 Mott outpost, insiders head for the 3rd-floor dining room.

Tai Hong Lau S   ▽ 20 | 11 | 12 | $23
70 Mott St. (bet. Bayard & Canal Sts.), 212-219-1431
◪ "Crowded" Cantonese offering "excellent" cooking and "good dim sum" "without pushcarts"; still, "communication is a problem", and both "decor and service aren't great – even by Chinatown standards."

40   www.zagat.com

Restaurants F | D | S | C

Taormina ◐ⓢ 20 | 17 | 19 | $42
147 Mulberry St. (bet. Grand & Hester Sts.), 212-219-1007
■ "Respectable food" arrives at "respectable prices" at this Little Italy "standby", formerly a John Gotti haunt that "now appeals to the tourist crowd"; red sauce "to die for" and interesting "people-watching" sum it up well.

Tennessee Mountain ⓢ 16 | 12 | 15 | $29
143 Spring St. (Wooster St.), 212-431-3993
◪ It's "hard to believe" this "backwoods" BBQ has put down roots in SoHo, but "hillbilly" fans "pretend" they're in the hollow and "wallow" in "big ol' slabs of ribs"; critics contend that this "Jersey-esque approach", albeit inexpensive, is about as authentic as "New England clam chowder in Memphis."

T.G.I. Friday's 11 | 11 | 12 | $24
47 Broadway (Exchange Pl.), 212-483-8322
◪ For "fast" eating, this Financial District brew 'n' burger "tourist trap" is a step above "Mickey D's", but for most, it's a "last resort" offering "heartburn-on-a-plate" chow and "slower-than-a-snail service" at "expensive-for-what-it-is" tabs; in sum, "spare yourself."

Thai House Cafe ⌿ 21 | 10 | 17 | $23
151 Hudson St. (Hubert St.), 212-334-1085
■ An "out-of-the-way location near the Holland Tunnel" doesn't keep those "stuck in traffic" away from this "killer" TriBeCa Thai and its "spicy kicks"; though the decor may be running on empty, pre-OPEC pricing allows for "affordable" fill-ups.

Thailand Restaurant ⓢ 23 | 11 | 15 | $22
106 Bayard St. (bet. Baxter & Mulberry Sts.), 212-349-3132
■ Famed for its "court-crowd lunch" scene, this "popular" Chinatown Thai offers food so "amazing" that some "want to be called for jury duty" just for the proximity; though "disheveled" decor is a turnoff, "how-can-you-go-wrong?" prices are turn-ons.

Thom ◐ⓢ – | – | – | E
60 Thompson Hotel, 60 Thompson St. (bet. Broome & Spring Sts.), 212-219-2000
On the ground floor of the new 60 Thompson Hotel, this SoHo stunner from the owners of Bond Street and Indochine seamlessly fuses the familiar with the exotic, adding vibrant Asian flavors (lemongrass, tamarind) to a seafood-focused American-Eclectic menu; it's sleek and seductive, from the low-lit, loungey interior to the eye-candy staff and leggy, Manolo-shod clientele.

Tja! ◐ⓢ ▽ 20 | 21 | 17 | $45
301 Church St. (Walker St.), 212-226-8900
■ The name "sounds strange" but the "food's tasty" at this TriBeCa fusion of Scandinavian and Asian cuisine –

www.zagat.com 41

Restaurants F D S C

yes, that's right – that also offers the "unique" option of "ordering the entire menu in appetizer sizes"; more to the point, there's a raging, "flavor-of-the-month" "bar scene" overseen by "hot hostesses with an attitude."

Torch ●S 20 | 23 | 18 | $42
137 Ludlow St. (bet. Rivington & Stanton Sts.), 212-228-5151
■ This "smoldering" Lower East Side take on a "'40s nightclub" feels like a cross between a swank "dinner party and an awards show"; look for "solid" French–South American fare, live music ranging from jazz to "accordion players" and a "Downtown swingers" crowd – and remember that "pushy" service comes with the territory.

Tribeca Grill S 22 | 21 | 21 | $53
375 Greenwich St. (Franklin St.), 212-941-3900
☑ "You're in good hands" at Robert De Niro and Drew Nieporent's "creative" New American veteran in TriBeCa that's "still flying" when it comes to "glorious food" in a handsome setting; conversationalists complain it's so "loud" that you should "go with someone to whom you have nothing to say", or just join the jumping bar scene.

Triple Eight Palace S 19 | 11 | 13 | $23
88 E. Broadway (bet. Division & Market Sts.), 212-941-8886
■ "Be adventurous and you'll be rewarded" at this cheap, "massive" Chinatown "feast palace" specializing in Hong Kong–style dim sum; be prepared for "garish" decor and "long lines" – and "bring a local or the best carts will pass you by."

27 Sunrise Seafood ●S – | – | – | M
27 Division St. (bet. Bowery & Market St.), 212-219-8498
Huge tanks in the window swimming with eels, lobsters and other sea creatures beckon one to this Chinatown seafood palace; the typical banquet-hall setting may not separate it from the competition, but the cooked-to-your-preference, ultra-fresh seafood does.

Va Tutto! S 19 | 18 | 17 | $38
23 Cleveland Pl. (bet. Kenmare & Spring Sts.), 212-941-0286
☑ "Cut-above-average" Little Italy Northern Italian with a "tranquil" garden, "delightful" fare and "affordable" tabs; though some call it the "coziest in the city", others lament a chef shift and say "service is slower than a trip to Rome."

Vegetarian Paradise S 20 | 11 | 15 | $18
33-35 Mott St. (Canal St.), 212-406-6988
☑ "Perfect imitations of meat" rendered in tofu ("faux chicken", "fake duck") "please the eye and palate" at this Chinatown Chinese-Vegetarian; although "cheap", the "atmosphere's not that good", so many "get it to go."

www.zagat.com

Restaurants | F | D | S | C |

Vietnam S
22 | 8 | 15 | $20

11-13 Doyers St. (bet. Bowery & Pell St.), 212-693-0725
■ "Stellar" dishes "bursting with flavor" await the "courageous" connoisseurs who're willing to brave this Chinatown Vietnamese's "spotty service" and "dingy", "subterranean" locale; though "far short of fine dining", an "epic menu" at "bargain prices" is compensation enough for most.

Vine
23 | 21 | 20 | $52

25 Broad St. (Exchange Pl.), 212-344-8463
■ The "food's di-Vine" at this Wall Street–area New American with an equally heavenly setting overlooking the NYSE; don't miss the blue-chip "private dining spaces" set in subterranean, refurbished "bank vaults."

Walker's ● S
20 | 17 | 17 | $26

16 N. Moore St. (Varick St.), 212-941-0142
■ TriBeCans savor "what's left of the old neighborhood" at this "trend-proof", circa 1890 "old NY" tavern where "superior bar food" comes at rock-bottom tabs; though some are "underwhelmed" by the "chirpy" service, the "low-key" vibe is hard to beat.

Wo Hop ● S ⊄
20 | 7 | 13 | $17

17 Mott St. (Canal St.), 212-267-2536
■ This 24/7 Chinatown "slumming" "classic" has been dishing out "dependable" eats since LaGuardia was mayor; sure, it's a "crowded" "dump" and dubious for "delicate digestive systems", so "close your eyes" and think of the "ridiculously low prices" instead.

Wong Kee S ⊄
23 | 7 | 12 | $17

113 Mott St. (bet. Canal & Hester Sts.), 212-966-1160
■ The good news is that this "fantastic" Chinatown Cantonese delivers "superb food" at "bargain basement" "'70s prices", but not so good are a "grumpy" staff and "zero atmosphere" where "everything's Formica"; diehards insist "don't look", just eat.

Woo Lae Oak S
22 | 21 | 19 | $43

148 Mercer St. (bet. Houston & Prince Sts.), 212-925-8200
◪ Given the "chic", "slick" surroundings, this SoHo Korean just may be the "hippest" of its genre; purists protest its "timid" menu and not-so-timid prices but agree the "trendy" bar scene can be amusing.

Wyanoka ●
∇ 23 | 20 | 21 | $41

173½ Mott St. (bet. Broome & Grand Sts.), 212-941-8757
■ Way "out of the way" in Little Italy lies this hepcat-friendly New American–Eclectic; "if you can find it", expect a "funky" crowd, "hip music", a "charming" staff and "inventive", "wonderful food" that runs a "close second to the great vibe."

---

www.zagat.com 43

Restaurants F | D | S | C

XO Kitchen 🅂⊘ ▽ 19 | 11 | 14 | $18
148 Hester St. (bet. Bowery & Elizabeth St.), 212-965-8645
96 Walker St. (bet. Centre & Lafayette Sts.), 212-343-8339
Off-the-beaten-path, quirky Chinatown finds, these funky, "always-crowded", Hong Kong–style joints resemble dingy rec rooms; their adventurous menus offer "great variety", which can be a problem, since some find it "hard to figure out what's good" and what's simply strange.

Zoë 🅂 22 | 20 | 20 | $47
90 Prince St. (bet. B'way & Mercer St.), 212-966-6722
■ Long a "SoHo standard", this "polished", open-kitchen New American is "still cranking", turning out "fresh, crisp" fare paired with a "seriously good" all-American wine list in "airy", "California-style" digs; though "kind of expensive", there's "never a dull moment" here.

Zutto 🅂 21 | 17 | 17 | $36
77 Hudson St. (Harrison St.), 212-233-3287
◪ "Primo sushi" "without the hassle" of fancier raw fisheries is yours at this TriBeCa Japanese that's a "best-kept secret" in the neighborhood; however, it may not be for long, as more and more boosters tout its "serene setting" and "rare affordability."

Restaurant Indexes

CUISINES
LOCATIONS
SPECIAL FEATURES

Indexes list the best of many within each category.

Restaurant Cuisine Index

CUISINES

American (New)
Blue Ribbon
Bridge Cafe
Cafe Colonial
Canteen
Cub Room
Duane Park Cafe
Edwards
Essex Restaurant
55 Wall
Grace
Harbour Lights
Harrison
Herban Kitchen
Juniper Café
Mercer Kitchen
Onieal's Grand St.
Pfiff
Rialto
Screening Room
71 Clinton Fresh Food
Stella
Thom
Tribeca Grill
Vine
Wyanoka
Zoë

American (Regional)
Hudson River Club

American (Traditional)
AKA Cafe
American Park
Bar 89
Bayard's
Broome St. Bar
Bubby's
City Hall
Fanelli's Cafe
Fraunces Tavern
Gallery, The
Grill Room
Houlihan's
Independent, The
Jerry's
Kitchenette
Odeon
Soho Steak
St. Maggie's Cafe
T.G.I. Friday's
Walker's

Argentinean
Novecento
Sosa Borella

Asian
Cendrillon
Kelley & Ping
Obeca Li
Roy's NY
Tja!

Australian
Eight Mile Creek

Austrian
Danube

Bakeries
Balthazar
Le Pain Quotidien
Once Upon a Tart

Barbecue
Tennessee Mountain

Belgian
Le Pain Quotidien
Petite Abeille

Brasserie
Balthazar
City Hall

Brazilian
Cafe Colonial

Caribbean
Cabana Nuevo Latino

Chinese
Au Mandarin
Big Wong
Canton
Dim Sum Go Go
Evergreen Shanghai
Excellent Dumpling House
Funky Broome
Golden Unicorn
Goody's
Grand Sichuan
Great NY Noodle Town
HSF
Joe's Shanghai

Restaurant Cuisine Index

Kam Chueh
Lili's Noodle Shop & Grill
Mandarin Court
New Green Bo
Nice Restaurant
Oriental Garden
Peking Duck House
Ping's Seafood
Shanghai Cuisine
Sweet-n-Tart
Tai Hong Lau
Triple Eight Palace
27 Sunrise Seafood
Vegetarian Paradise
Wo Hop
Wong Kee
XO Kitchen

Coffeehouses/Desserts
Ferrara
Once Upon a Tart
Starbucks

Cuban
Cabana Nuevo Latino
Café Habana
Paladar

Delis/Sandwich Shops
Cosi
Grilled Cheese NYC
Hampton Chutney Co.
Katz's Delicatessen

Dim Sum
Dim Sum Go Go
Golden Unicorn
HSF
Mandarin Court
Nice Restaurant
Ping's Seafood
Sweet-n-Tart
Tai Hong Lau
Triple Eight Palace
27 Sunrise Seafood
Vegetarian Paradise

Eclectic/International
Barrio
Blue Ribbon
Cupping Room Cafe
Ivy's Bistro
Kitchen Club
Rice
Thom
Wyanoka

Egyptian
Casa La Femme

Ethiopian
Ghenet

Filipino
Cendrillon

French
Bayard's
Chanterelle
L'Ecole
Le Gamin
L'Orange Bleue
Mercer Kitchen
Montrachet
Torch

French (Bistro)
Alison on Dominick
Balthazar
Bistro Les Amis
Bistrot Margot
Capsouto Frères
Chez Bernard
Country Cafe
Félix
Jean Claude
Le Jardin Bistro
Le Père Pinard
Le Pescadou
Le Zinc
Lucky Strike
Manhattan Bistro
Odeon
Provence
Raoul's
Soho Steak

French (New)
Bouley Bakery
14 Wall Street

Greek
Snack

Hamburgers
Broome St. Bar
City Hall
Fanelli Cafe
Houlihan's

www.zagat.com 47

Restaurant Cuisine Index

Health Food
Herban Kitchen
Spring Street Natural

Indian
Baluchi's
Hampton Chutney Co.
Namaskaar
Salaam Bombay

Italian
Acappella
Angelo's of Mulberry
Arqua
Bacco
Barolo
Bot
Da Nico
Ecco
Ferrara
F.illi Ponte
Gigino at Wagner Park
Gigino Trattoria
Il Corallo
Il Cortile
Il Fornaio
Il Giglio
Il Palazzo
I Tre Merli
La Mela
L'Ulivo Focacceria
Mezzogiorno
Mooza
Nello
Oro Blu
Peasant
Pellegrino's
Pepolino
Pepe Rosso
Positano Ristorante
Quartino
Roc
Sal Anthony's S.P.Q.R.
Savore
Scalini Fedeli
Sosa Borella
Taormina
Va Tutto!

Japanese
Ajisen Noodle
Blue Ribbon Sushi
Honmura An
Kitchen Club
Nobu
Obeca Li
Omen
Zutto

Jewish
Essex Restaurant
Katz's Delicatessen
Ratner's
Sammy's Roumanian

Korean
Clay
Kori
Woo Lae Oak

Malaysian
Ba Ba Malaysian
Nyonya
Penang

Mediterranean
Cafe Noir
Harrison, The
Layla
Mangia
Mooza
Savoy
Sirocco

Mexican/Tex-Mex
Burritoville
Café Habana
Casa Mexicana
El Teddy's
Mary Ann's
Mexican Radio

Middle Eastern
Layla

Moroccan
Country Cafe
L'Orange Bleue

Noodle Shops
Ajisen Noodle
Big Wong
Bo-Ky
Great NY Noodle Town
Honmura An
Kelley & Ping
Lili's Noodle Shop & Grill
Pho Bang
Pho Viet Huong

Restaurant Cuisine Index

Nuevo Latino
Cabana Nuevo Latino

Peruvian
Nobu

Pizza
Little Italy Pizza
Lombardi's
Pizzeria Uno Chicago

Portuguese
Pão!
Pico

Scandinavian
Good World B/G
Tja!

Seafood
American Park
Aquagrill
Harry's at Hanover Sq.
Kam Chueh
Lansky Lounge/Grill
Le Pescadou
Oriental Garden
Ping's Seafood
Roy's NY
27 Sunrise Seafood

Soups
Daily Soup

South American
Cabana Nuevo Latino
Ideya
Paladar
Torch

Southern/Soul
Bubby's

Spanish
AKA Cafe
Flor de Sol
1492 Food
Ñ
Oliva

Steakhouses
Delmonico's
Dylan Prime
Harry's at Hanover Sq.
Lansky Lounge
MarkJoseph
Soho Steak

Tapas
Café Noir
Flor de Sol
1492 Food
Ñ
Oliva

Thai
Kin Khao
Thai House Cafe
Thailand Restaurant

Turkish
Bereket

Vegetarian
Grilled Cheese NYC
Herban Kitchen
Vegetarian Paradise

Vietnamese
Bo-Ky
MeKong
Nam Phuong
New Pasteur
Nha Trang
Pho Bang
Pho Viet Huong
Vietnam

Restaurant Location Index

LOCATIONS

Chinatown
Ajisen Noodle
Ba Ba Malaysian
Big Wong
Bo-Ky
Canton
Dim Sum Go Go
Evergreen Shanghai
Excellent Dumpling
Golden Unicorn
Goody's
Grand Sichuan
Great NY Noodle Town
HSF
Joe's Shanghai
Kam Chueh
Mandarin Court
New Green Bo
New Pasteur
Nha Trang
Nice Restaurant
Oriental Garden
Peking Duck Hse.
Pho Bang
Pho Viet Huong
Ping's
Shanghai Cuisine
Sweet-n-Tart Cafe
Tai Hong Lau
Thailand Rest.
Triple Eight
27 Sunrise Seafood
Vegetarian Paradise
Vietnam
Wo Hop
Wong Kee
XO Kitchen

Financial District
American Park
Au Mandarin
Bayard's
Bridge Cafe
Burritoville
Cabana
Cosi Sandwich
Daily Soup
Delmonico's
55 Wall
14 Wall St.
Fraunces Tavern
Gigino at Wagner Park
Grill Room
Harbour Lights
Harry's Hanover Sq.
Houlihan's
Hudson River Club
Il Giglio
Lili's Noodle Shop
Little Italy
Mangia
MarkJoseph
Pizzeria Uno
Quartino
Roy's NY
Starbucks
St. Maggie's Cafe
T.G.I. Friday's
Vine

Little Italy
Angelo's
Bistrot Margot
Bot
Cafe Colonial
Café Habana
Clay
Da Nico
Eight Mile Creek
Ferrara
Funky Broome
Ghenet
Il Cortile
Il Fornaio
Il Palazzo
Kitchen Club
La Mela
Le Jardin
Lombardi's
MeKong
Mexican Radio
Nyonya
Onieal's
Peasant
Pellegrino's
Pho Bang
Positano
Rialto
Rice
Sal's S.P.Q.R.
Taormina
Va Tutto!
Wyanoka

Restaurant Location Index

Lower East Side
AKA Cafe
Barrio
Bereket
Casa Mexicana
Essex Rest.
1492 Food
Good World B/G
Grilled Cheese
Katz's Deli
Lansky Lounge/Grill
Le Père Pinard
Mooza
Oliva
Paladar
Ratner's
Sammy's Roumanian
71 Clinton Fresh Food
Torch

SoHo
Alison on Dominick
Aquagrill
Bacco
Balthazar
Baluchi's
Bar 89
Barolo
Bistro Les Amis
Blue Ribbon
Blue Ribbon Sushi
Broome St. Bar
Cafe Noir
Canteen
Casa La Femme
Cendrillon
Chez Bernard
Country Cafe
Cub Room
Cupping Room Cafe
Fanelli's Cafe
Félix
Gallery, The
Hampton Chutney Co.
Herban Kitchen
Honmura An
Ideya
Il Corallo
I Tre Merli
Jean Claude
Jerry's
Kelley & Ping
Kin Khao
L'Ecole
Le Gamin
Le Pain Quotidien
Le Pescadou
Little Italy Pizza
L'Orange Bleue
Lucky Strike
L'Ulivo
Manhattan Bistro
Mercer Kitchen
Mezzogiorno
Ñ
Namaskaar
Nello
Novecento
Omen
Once Upon a Tart
Oro Blu
Pão!
Penang
Pepe Rosso
Pfiff
Provence
Quilty's
Raoul's
Savore
Savoy
Sirocco
Snack
Soho Steak
Spring St. Natural
Starbucks
Stella
Tennessee Mtn.
Thom
Woo Lae Oak
Zoë

TriBeCa
Acappella
Arqua
Bouley Bakery
Bubby's
Capsouto Frères
Chanterelle
City Hall
Danube
Duane Park Cafe
Dylan Prime
Ecco
Edward's
El Teddy's
F.illi Ponte
Flor de Sol
Gigino

www.zagat.com   51

Restaurant Location Index

Grace
Harrison, The
Independent, The
Ivy's Bistro
Juniper Cafe
Kitchenette
Kori
Layla
Le Zinc
Mary Ann's
Montrachet
Nam Phuong
Nino's
Nobu
Obeca Li
Odeon
Pepolino
Petite Abeille
Pico
Roc
Salaam Bombay
Scalini Fedeli
Screening Room
Sosa Borella
Starbucks
Thai House Cafe
Tja!
Tribeca Grill
Walker's
Zutto

Restaurant Special Feature Index

SPECIAL FEATURES

Business Dining
Acappella
Bouley Bakery
City Hall
Danube
Delmonico's
Duane Park Cafe
Ecco
55 Wall
14 Wall Street
Fraunces Tavern
Harry's/Hanover Sq.
L'Ecole
Nobu
Oro Blu
Roy's New York
St. Maggie's Cafe
Tribeca Grill
Vine

Historic Places
(* building only)
1763 Fraunces Tavern
1794 Bridge Cafe*
1863 City Hall*
1872 Fanelli's Cafe*
1875 Harry's/Hanover Sq.
1888 Katz's Deli
1890 Walker's
1891 Delmonico's
1892 Ferrara
1905 Ratner's
1938 Wo Hop

"In" Places
Alison on Dominick
Aquagrill
Balthazar
Bar 89
Bayard's
Blue Ribbon
Bot
Bouley Bakery
Café Habana
Canteen
Capsouto Frères
Cub Room
Danube
Dim Sum Go Go
Eight Mile Creek
Gallery, The
Grace
Harrison, The
Le Zinc
Mercer Kitchen
Nello
Nobu
Odeon
Peasant
Pico
Raoul's
71 Clinton Fresh Food
Thom
Tja!
Wyanoka
Zoë

Jury Duty
(Best bets near courthouses)
Arqua
Ba Ba Malaysian
Bo-Ky
Bouley Bakery
Bridge Cafe
City Hall
Da Nico
Danube
Duane Park Cafe
Ecco
Excellent Dumpling
Goody's
Great NY Noodle House
Il Cortile
Il Fornaio
Il Palazzo
Joe's Shanghai
Kitchenette
L'Ecole
Lombardi's
Nam Phuong
New Green Bo
New Pasteur
Nha Trang
Nobu
Odeon
Oriental Garden
Pho Viet Huong
Roc
Sal Anthony's SPQR
Sweet-n-Tart
Taormina
Thailand Rest.
Vietnam

www.zagat.com 53

Restaurant Special Feature Index

Wo Hop
Wong Kee

Noteworthy Newcomers
Ajisen Noodle
AKA Cafe
Edward's
Essex
1492 Food
Gallery, The
Harrison, The
Le Zinc
MarkJoseph
Mooza
Nello
Paladar
Pfiff
Pico
Quartino
Sirocco
Thom
27 Sunrise Seafood
Wyanoka

Power Scenes
Balthazar
Bayard's
Bouley Bakery
City Hall
Danube
Delmonico's
55 Wall
Nobu
Tribeca Grill
Vine

Private Rooms
Alison on Dominick
American Park
Angelo's of Mulberry
Au Mandarin
Bacco
Barolo
Barrio
Bayard's
Bouley Bakery
Bubby's
Canteen
City Hall
Cub Room
Da Nico
Danube
Delmonico's
Dylan Prime

Eight Mile Creek
El Teddy's
Essex
F.illi Ponte
14 Wall Street
Golden Unicorn
Grill Room
Harbour Lights
Harrison, The
Harry's/Hanover Sq.
Hudson River Club
Il Cortile
Il Palazzo
Independent, The
I Tre Merli
Kitchen Club
La Mela
Lansky Lounge
Mexican Radio
Montrachet
Nobu
Novecento
Obeca Li
Odeon
Onieal's Grand St.
Oriental Garden
Pão!
Peking Duck House
Pepolino
Pico
Positano Ristorante
Provence
Raoul's
Ratner's
Rialto
Sal Anthony's SPQR
Sammy's Roumanian
Savore
Savoy
Scalini Fedeli
Screening Room
St. Maggie's Cafe
Tennessee Mountain
Tja!
Tribeca Grill
Va Tutto!
Vine
Walker's
Woo Lae Oak
Wyanoka

Romantic Places
Alison on Dominick
Balthazar

Restaurant Special Feature Index

Barolo
Capsouto Frères
Casa La Femme
Chanterelle
Cub Room
Danube
Dylan Prime
Flor de Sol
Honmura An
Le Jardin Bistro
Novecento
Pico
Provence
Raoul's
Rialto
Savoy
Screening Room
Sirocco
Torch
Va Tutto!

Visitors on Expense Account
Acappella
Bayard's
Bouley Bakery
Chanterelle
City Hall
Danube
Delmonico's
F.illi Ponte
Il Cortile
Il Giglio
MarkJoseph

Montrachet
Nello
Nobu
Pico
Roc
Scalini Fedeli
Vine

Winning Wine Lists
Alison on Dominick
Aquagrill
Balthazar
Barolo
Bayard's
Blue Ribbon
Bouley Bakery
Capsouto Frères
Chanterelle
City Hall
Cub Room
Danube
F.illi Ponte
Harry's/Hanover Sq.
I Tre Merli
L'Ecole
Mercer Kitchen
Montrachet
Ñ
Provence
Raoul's
Savoy
Scalini Fedeli
Tribeca Grill
Zoë

Nightlife

Nightlife Map

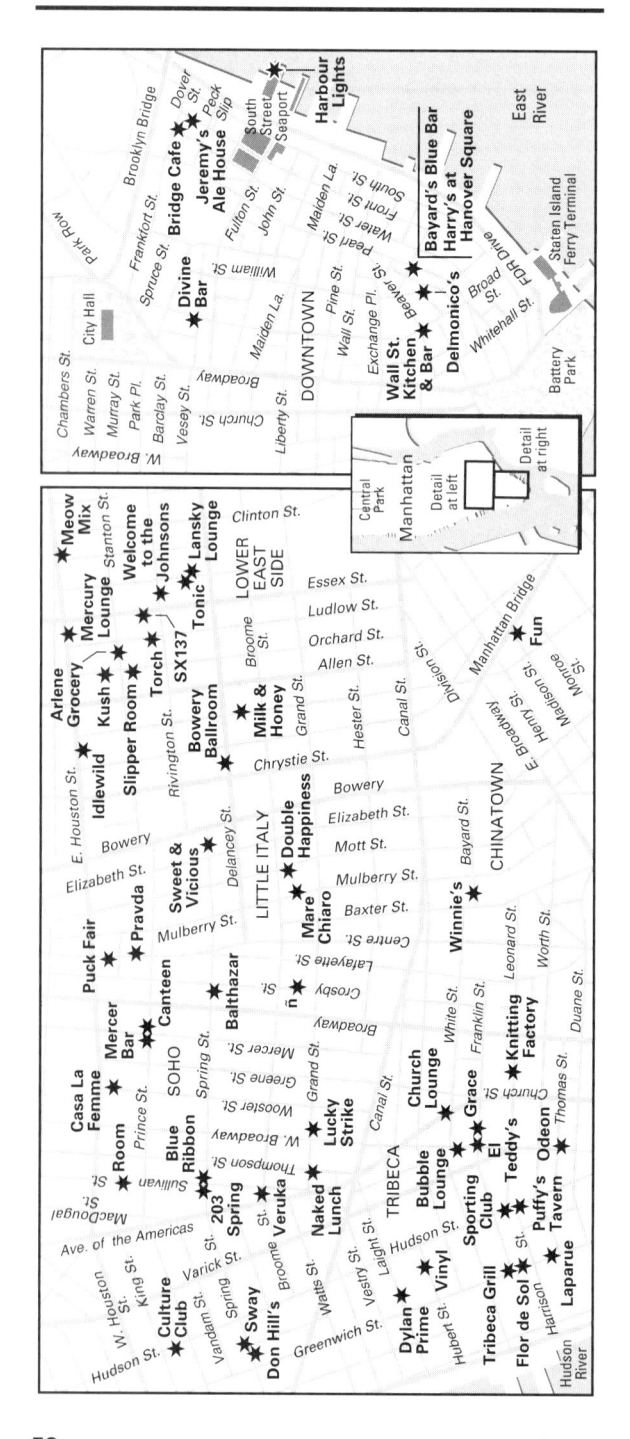

Top Rated Nightlife Spots

Listed in order of Appeal rating, excluding places with low votes.

Top by Category

Overall Appeal
- 26 Church Lounge
- 25 Milk and Honey
  Flor de Sol
  Dylan Prime
- 24 Chibi's Sake Bar
  Casa La Femme

Decor
- 26 Church Lounge
- 25 Casa La Femme
  Dylan Prime
  Kush
  Idlewild
  Grand Bar

Service
- 27 Milk and Honey
- 24 Eight Mile Creek
- 22 Delmonico's
  Chibi's Sake Bar
  Bayard's Blue Bar*
  Savoy

Bars
- 25 Milk and Honey
  Flor de Sol
  Dylan Prime
- 24 Chibi's Sake Bar
  Balthazar
  Good World B/G

Coffeehouses
- 23 Cafe Gitane
  Lotus Cafe
- 21 Kavehaz
  Pink Pony Cafe
- 20 Scharmann's
- 19 Cupping Room Cafe

Dance Clubs
- 24 Vinyl
- 21 RM
  S.O.B.'s
- 20 NV/289 Lounge
  Shine
- 19 Culture Club

Lounges
- 26 Church Lounge
- 24 Casa La Femme
  Savoy
  Grand Bar
- 23 Kush
  Sugar

Music Clubs
- 22 Bowery Ballroom
- 21 Knitting Factory
  Tonic
- 19 Mercury Lounge
  Living Room
  Arlene Grocery

Top by Neighborhood

Financial District
- 23 Delmonico's
- 22 Divine Bar
  Bayard's Blue Bar
  Harbour Lights
- 21 Bridge Cafe
  55 Wall

Little Italy
- 24 Chibi's Sake Bar
- 23 Cafe Gitane
  Eight Mile Creek
  Double Happiness
  Peasant
- 22 Pravda

Lower East Side
- 25 Milk and Honey
- 24 Good World B/G
- 23 Kush
  Torch
  Lotus Cafe
- 22 Bowery Ballroom

SoHo
- 24 Casa La Femme
  Balthazar
  Savoy
  Grand Bar
  Raoul's
- 23 N

TriBeCa
- 26 Church Lounge
- 25 Flor de Sol
  Dylan Prime
- 24 Vinyl
- 23 Grace
  Tribeca Grill

---

* Tied with the place listed directly above it

www.zagat.com

Key to Ratings/Symbols

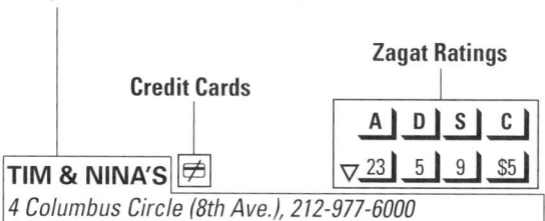

Name, Address & Phone Number

Credit Cards

Zagat Ratings

A	D	S	C
▽ 23	5	9	$5

TIM & NINA'S ⌀
4 Columbus Circle (8th Ave.), 212-977-6000

◩ Open 7 days a week, 24 hours a day, this "deep dive" bar with a bathroom and phone booth across the street looks like a "none-too-clean garage" (but don't tell the health department); however, "dirt cheap" prices, a free-flowing tap and unlimited pretzels gratis draw "spaced-out crowds" of "multi-pierced patrons"; P.S. don't trip on any of the customers on your way out.

Review, with surveyors' comments in quotes

Nightspots with the highest overall ratings and greatest popularity and importance are printed in CAPITAL LETTERS.

Before each review a symbol indicates whether responses were uniform ■ or mixed ◩.

Credit Cards: ⌀ no credit cards accepted

Ratings: Appeal, Decor and Service are rated on a scale of **0** to **30**. The Cost (C) column reflects surveyors' estimated price of a typical single drink.

A Appeal	**D** Decor	**S** Service	**C** Cost
23	5	9	$5

- **0–9** poor to fair
- **10–15** fair to good
- **16–19** good to very good
- **20–25** very good to excellent
- **26–30** extraordinary to perfection
- ▽ low response/less reliable

A place listed without ratings is either an important **newcomer** or a popular **write-in**. For such places, the estimated cost is indicated by the following symbols.

- **I** Below $4
- **M** $4 to $7
- **E** $8 to $10
- **VE** More Than $10

www.zagat.com

Nightlife | A | D | S | C |

Angel | 21 | 19 | 18 | $7 |
174 Orchard St. (bet. E. Houston & Stanton Sts.), 212-780-0313
■ "Sleek" decor rendered in "dreamy" shades of blue lends some "romance" to this Lower East Side bar/lounge, while its "extremely high ceiling" helps transcend its "too-narrow" layout; regulars recommend the second floor perch for "good people-watching" but admit the crowd (like the music) "varies nightly" and can be "hit or miss."

Anotheroom | 22 | 20 | 20 | $7 |
249 W. Broadway (bet. Beach & N. Moore Sts.), 212-226-1418
■ "No pretension" is evident at this "out-of-the-way", "low-maintenance" TriBeCa bar where "superfriendly bartenders" dispense "only beer and wine" (just like its siblings, The Room and Otheroom); given the "small", "very chill" setting, it's more appropriate for "late-night, low-voiced chats" than for rowdy groups of "binge drinkers."

Antarctica | 15 | 12 | 18 | $5 |
287 Hudson St. (Spring St.), 212-352-1666
■ "Down-to-earth" SoHo "dive bar" that's best known for its nightly 'name game' ("you drink gratis" if "your name is posted" in the window); otherwise, it's "spacious", verging on "austere", with "not much charm", though musicologists say the "kick-ass jukebox" is pretty darn "great."

Arlene Grocery ∌ | 19 | 11 | 14 | $5 |
95 Stanton St. (bet. Ludlow & Orchard Sts.), 212-358-1633
■ For a "low-risk way (both time- and moneywise)" to check out "unsigned bands", try this "no-frills, straight on" Lower East Side club that thrills its "grungy" crowd with "cheap drinks and inventive music", "usually with no cover charge"; despite a "recent expansion", it's just as "sweaty" and "tightly packed" as before, particularly for Monday night's popular "punk rock karaoke."

Baby Doll Lounge | 17 | 11 | 14 | $6 |
34 White St. (Church St.), 212-226-4870
☒ "As sleazy as it should be", this "hip" strip club is a "classic" stop when you're out "slumming" in TriBeCa, but oglers groan that since the front-room dolls have "their tops on", it's "no fun" anymore; even though the back is a bit racier, the cry still goes up: "put it back on."

BALTHAZAR | 24 | 23 | 20 | $9 |
80 Spring St. (bet. B'way & Crosby St.), 212-965-1414
■ "Sophistication oozes" from Keith McNally's "still-hopping" SoHo French brasserie, the "last civilized place in NY", where you can rub elbows with "blondes in black", "modelizers" and "movie stars breezing through" ("hi, Gwyneth!"); granted, some say it's "better for dinner than drinks" and you might "need De Niro's bank account" to settle the check, but for an "ego boost" or a round of "name that celebrity", this one's hard to beat.

Nightlife A | D | S | C

BAR 89   22 | 24 | 17 | $8
89 Mercer St. (bet. Broome & Spring Sts.), 212-274-0989
■ Coed "space-age bathrooms" give "see and be seen" a new meaning at this "sleek" SoHo lounge, whose transparent stall doors "fog up" only after you "latch" them; in addition to the "legendary" loos, patrons pronounce the potables "nice", if "expensive", and moan it's "a pity about the service."

Barramundi ⇗   21 | 19 | 19 | $6
147 Ludlow St. (bet. Rivington & Stanton Sts.), 212-529-6900
■ "Hip and relaxed without inducing eye-rolling", this Lower East Side lounge is done up in "Adirondack-funk" style that might be a bit "creepy" to some, but its secret weapons are a "real working fireplace" in the back and a "hidden", "killer garden" even farther back; fussy drinkers say a "ginger martini never disappoints" at this "diamond in the rough."

Bayard's Blue Bar   22 | 23 | 22 | $9
1 Hanover Sq. (bet. Pearl & Stone Sts.), 212-514-9454
■ "Wall Street suits" repair to this "very quiet" Financial District bar/restaurant set in the landmark India House, knowing they can count on "class, comfort and smooth drinks" before moving on to the dining room for some of chef Eberhard Mueller's cooking; outgoing types wonder "where is everyone?"

Beckett's Bar & Grill   17 | 14 | 20 | $6
78 Pearl St. (Broad St.), 212-269-1001
■ "Perfect for drinks with Goldman Sachs traders" or "former frat boys", this "friendly Irish pub" in the Financial District keeps happy-hour habitués happy thanks to a variety of draft beers served by a staff with "accents galore"; maybe the "food's not great", but that's not what this "hangout" is all about.

Blarney Stone   11 | 9 | 14 | $5
11 Trinity Pl. (Morris St.), 212-269-4988
☒ "Men who act as if they've never seen a woman before" warm the stools of this Financial District "quick fix-me-up" Irish pub that's a "best bet to get drunk cheaply" – just "make sure you have a hard hat, tool belt or plumber's butt to fit in."

Blue Ribbon   23 | 20 | 21 | $8
97 Sullivan St. (bet. Prince & Spring Sts.), 212-274-0404
■ Score "clams on the half shell and a bottle of Merlot at 2 AM" at this "hip" and "happening" SoHo restaurant/bar that's renowned as a late-late scene and after-work "chef's hang"; irregulars claim it's "very regulars-oriented", but no matter how often you show up, it's "hard to get a space at the bar", given the "tight" setup and the drawing power of its "cutie-patootie", "movie star bartenders."

Nightlife <u>A</u> <u>D</u> <u>S</u> <u>C</u>

bOb <u>21</u> <u>15</u> <u>16</u> <u>$6</u>
235 Eldridge St. (bet. Houston & Stanton Sts.), 212-777-0588
■ This "packed" Lower East Side "shoebox" is "proof that all meat markets aren't on the Upper East Side", given the number of "alpha males" getting up close and personal with "girls in vintage clothes"; it's "impossible to move" on weekends with all the "sweaty" bodies, "bumping" and "grinding like coffee beans."

Boom <u>18</u> <u>17</u> <u>16</u> <u>$8</u>
152 Spring St. (bet. Wooster & W. B'way), 212-431-3663
◪ SoHo's "pretty people" strap on their "best stilettos" to prove the "tables are strong enough to dance on" at this "dark" restaurant/club where the DJs and live acts blast jazzy beats for a crowd comprised of "more Euros than the UN"; though a few '90s scenesters sense this "old hangout" has gone bust, "Julia Stiles wanna-bes" with "French haircuts" still breeze by and are always welcome.

Botanica Bar ⌀ <u>19</u> <u>15</u> <u>18</u> <u>$6</u>
47 E. Houston St. (bet. Mott & Mulberry Sts.), 212-343-7251
■ The "subterranean locale" seems to suit the "hip", latter-day flower children planted on "comfy couches" (à la previous tenant the Knitting Factory) at this "gritty, casual pit stop" off the beaten track on East Houston, where "shaggy NoLita types" show up to "start the night."

BOWERY BALLROOM <u>22</u> <u>18</u> <u>16</u> <u>$6</u>
6 Delancey St. (bet. Bowery & Chrystie St.), 212-533-2111
■ "Catch one of your heroes" of the alternative scene at this "hopping" Lower East Side concert space where the "upstairs/downstairs" setup features "awesome" balconies with "great sight lines" down to the expansive main floor, plus a basement bar where fans "mingle with the bands" over a "reasonable" drink or three; it's cited by many a rock 'n' roll junkie as "best in class for live tunes."

Bridge Cafe <u>21</u> <u>19</u> <u>20</u> <u>$7</u>
279 Water St. (Dover St.), 212-227-3344
■ Obscured in the shadow of the Brooklyn Bridge, this "remote" "hideaway" is an easily overlooked guardian of "quaint" "old NY" – as it should be, having first opened its doors as a wine merchant in 1794; cognoscenti call it a "quiet", "comfortable" haunt where the ethic is still "eat, lounge" and be merry.

Broome Street Bar <u>18</u> <u>16</u> <u>19</u> <u>$6</u>
363 W. Broadway (Broome St.), 212-925-2086
■ Perhaps being "real and reliable in SoHo" is no great feat, but this "old-fashioned" "burger-and-beer" purveyor still sweeps the field as an underachiever's "haven in the land of the trendy"; in this nabe, tipping a jar in "downscale" digs with a "nice corner view" qualifies as a "rare treat."

www.zagat.com

Nightlife   A | D | S | C

BUBBLE LOUNGE   22 | 22 | 17 | $9
228 W. Broadway (bet. Franklin & White Sts.), 212-431-3433
■ "Impress your date" with the red velvet, "roses and champagne" at this "classy" TriBeCa scene stealer where the "awesome" selection of bubbly beguiles "giddy" "twentysomething" "Wall Street" types into thinking that "money is no object"; some mutter it "used to be cooler" before the "B&T" "hairdos" and "toupees" popped up, but consensus says it will "never go out of style."

Cafe Gitane ⊅   23 | 20 | 17 | $7
242 Mott St. (bet. Houston & Prince Sts.), 212-334-9552
■ Put "your best French accent" to the test at this "trendy" NoLita "refuge" for the "truly fabulous" and the "impossibly gorgeous", who keep busy checking themselves out in the "scarily huge wall mirror"; its Gallic habitués are easily identified by their "goatees" and "filterless cigarettes."

Cafe Noir   21 | 19 | 17 | $7
32 Grand St. (Thompson St.), 212-431-7910
■ Rick's Cafe Americain it will never be, but this "cool", "Moroccan-style oasis", a SoHo tribute to "downscale chic", provides plenty of that "dark and sultry" thing to supplement its tapas and "excellent sangria"; its "lively" clientele squeezes in for "late-night drinks and eats", and everyone shows up with "at least one pack" of smokes.

Canteen   22 | 23 | 18 | $9
142 Mercer St., downstairs (Prince St.), 212-431-7676
■ "*Clockwork Orange* goes new millennium" and SoHo's "hypersassy" set goes underground at this "very cool" basement mess hall/bar, known for its "high hip factor" and "groovy", retina-melting decor; the "bright" look attracts "lots of models" whose "head-to-toe Dolce & Gabbana" goes head-to-head with the neon hues of "those chairs!"

CASA LA FEMME   24 | 25 | 18 | $9
150 Wooster St. (bet. Houston & Prince Sts.), 212-505-0005
■ Adventurers are "transported" to chez "Scheherazade" at this "sexy" SoHo restaurant/lounge decked out in a "kitschy" Egyptian style replete with "tents, hookahs and big floor pillows" artfully strewn about; belly dancers reminiscent of "upscale lap dancers" put on a "sensuous" show, and though some quarrel about the "overpriced drinks", there's no de-nile it's definitely "different."

Chibi's Sake Bar   24 | 19 | 22 | $8
238 Mott St. (bet. Prince & Spring Sts.), 212-274-0054
■ This "funky find" "next to the Kitchen Club" in NoLita is a "small, cozy" spot to "sit for a few hours" and sip sake served every conceivable way ("who knew there were so many kinds?"); the "mellow" mood is enhanced by "addictive" Franco-Japanese "munchies" as well as appearances by its namesake and "mascot", "Chibi the dog."

Nightlife | A | D | S | C |

CHURCH LOUNGE | 26 | 26 | 21 | $10 |
Tribeca Grand Hotel, 2 Sixth Ave. (White St.), 212-519-6600
■ Aptly named given the "beautiful interior architecture", this "swanky" sanctuary surrounded by the Tribeca Grand's eight-story atrium is a "happening" new "favorite" of a "hip Wall Street" congregation that's devoted to "see-and-be-seen" rituals; just "be sure to hit an ATM" first, or risk embarrassment when the collection plate comes around.

Circa Tabac | 22 | 21 | 20 | $8 |
32 Watts St. (Thompson St.), 212-941-1781
■ Devotees "love the atmosphere", though the air might be a bit thin, at this SoHo "smokers' sanctuary", which spans the globe to offer puffers over 200 brands of cigarettes and cheroots; a "cool idea" for loyalists of Lady Nicotine, it's also a safe bet for claustrophobes looking to "avoid crowds."

City Hall | 22 | 22 | 21 | $9 |
131 Duane St. (bet. Church St. & W. B'way), 212-227-7777
■ It's "spin city" at warp speed in the "candlelit", "grown-up" bar of this "classy" TriBeCan where "lots of suits" settle back on "leather seats", oozing "testosterone"; the scene is reminiscent of "old NY" in its "kinda pricey" prime – "Boss Tweed himself" would feel right at home here.

Cub Room | 21 | 21 | 19 | $8 |
131 Sullivan St. (Prince St.), 212-677-4100
■ Leave behind "the daily grind" at this "SoHo favorite", a "classy" eatery where cub "lawyers" and "brokers" bolt "first-rate" "watermelon martinis" in the "comfortable bar"; it's a "warm" lair with "big windows" and "lots of seating", and those who can bear the slightly "snooty" vibe call it "a definite must" for "meeting" and "mingling."

Culture Club | 19 | 17 | 14 | $7 |
179 Varick St. (bet. Charlton & King Sts.), 212-243-1999
◪ "Gen Xers" who are "not turned off by Wang Chung" still tumble for this SoHo "'80s flashback", a rilly rad "blast" of "vintage" dance tunes and decor from the Pac-Man era; though dissed as "overpriced", "sweaty" and terminally "tacky", it's a "guilty pleasure" and a rare chance to boogie "till you drop" on a floor "packed" with "Go-Go's"-crazed "bachelorettes" out to "have a ball."

Cupping Room Cafe | 19 | 18 | 18 | $7 |
359 W. Broadway (bet. Broome & Grand Sts.), 212-925-2898
■ As "warm" and "relaxed" as "granny's kitchen", this "pleasant, popular" SoHo "standby" is a place to "lie low" over "tea and cake" or get high with a "great Bloody Mary" in a bar decked out with "country" furnishings.

Cyber Cafe | ▽ | 16 | 15 | 16 | $6 |
273 Lafayette St. (Prince St.), 212-334-5140
◪ This SoHo coffeehouse is always online when jonesing "tech guys" "need Internet access" or a "cool" spot to "just

www.zagat.com 65

Nightlife A | D | S | C

hang" and get wired; beer, wine and munchies are now available, and users call it a "good idea" despite flames for the "aseptic" atmosphere – as if that counted in cyberspace.

Dakota Roadhouse ⌀   13 | 12 | 18 | $5
43 Park Pl. (bet. Church St. & W. B'way), 212-962-9800
■ With this downscale saloon just blocks away, City Hall's nine-to-fivers don't have to travel far to find an "ordinary bar" for "after-work drinks" on the "cheap"; it's more of a "men's place", boasting pool tables, junk food and a "good juke", though insiders insist the yank-a-lobster-from-the-tank game is really what "it's all about."

Delmonico's   23 | 24 | 22 | $8
56 Beaver St. (S. William St.), 212-509-1144
■ "Old-school Wall Street" wines and dines at this Financial District "institution" where "guys in suspenders" take stock of "business" over Chivas and cigars; oozing an "opulent" "mahogany" luster, it's a "quiet", "classy" destination and a standout on many an "expense account."

Denial   20 | 17 | 18 | $8
46 Grand St. (bet. Thompson St. & W. B'way), 212-925-9449
■ Rice wine buffs in search of a "quality" venue for sipping sake turn to this "loungey" SoHo bar with a doorman, DJs and dancing as nods to the "hip"; it's a "popular" scene, and even "cool" customers "can't deny" it's "lots of fun."

Diva   19 | 20 | 16 | $8
341 W. Broadway (bet. Broome & Grand Sts.), 212-941-9024
■ Think *Tosca* with "lots of SoHo attitude", and you'll get a sense of this "sleek", "dark" bar/restaurant where the "awesome Italian ambiance" is "romantic" and dramatically "different"; its floor-to-ceiling windows open up in *bel tempo*, adding a street dimension to the "great people-watching."

DIVINE BAR   22 | 21 | 19 | $8
55 Liberty St., 2nd fl. (bet. B'way & Nassau St.), 212-791-9463
■ "Meet a suit" over Beaujolais at this "sceney" oenophile "favorite" in the Financial District, which offers "wonderful" "wine tasting" from an "imaginative" list complemented by "delish tapas"; it's "very lively" and "crowded" with "yuppies at play", and a heavenly place to "hook up."

Donald Sacks   14 | 13 | 15 | $7
World Financial Ctr., 220 Vesey St. (West St.), 212-619-4600
◪ Maybe it's "not for nightlife" in the late-night sense, but this Financial District watering hole does the job as "happy-hour central" for "nonmillionaire" "corporate" sorts looking for an "escape" at the end of the trading day; set in the WFC courtyard, it's usually "not as crowded" as its nearby loosened-tie rivals; **N.B. closed at press time.**

Nightlife | A | D | S | C |

Don's Hill's | 17 | 11 | 15 | $6 |
511 Greenwich St. (Spring St.), 212-334-1390

■ Lodged in a dimly lit SoHo bunker, this "quirky" "bar–cum–dance club" features "hot live bands" and "hoppin'" "'80s party" nights that draw a "cool, diverse crowd" ranging from "drag queens" and "fashionistas" to "hipsters" and metalheads; in the true underground spirit, it's "ugly as hell" (maybe even "downright scary"), yet "full of character."

DOUBLE HAPPINESS | 23 | 20 | 16 | $7 |
173 Mott St. (bet. Broome & Grand Sts.), 212-941-1282

■ Looks like "the secret's out" about this "double cool" "underground" "hideaway" in Little Italy, a former "speakeasy" full of "private nooks" that's morphed into a "dark, seductive" "make-out bar"; crowd-pleasers include the "funky" "old Chinatown decor", "drum and bass" mood music and "amazing green-tea martinis", though scenesters sense it's growing "too popular" with "slumming" yups.

DYLAN PRIME | 25 | 25 | 22 | $9 |
62 Laight St. (Greenwich St.), 212-334-4783

■ Bringing it all back home to a "remote" part of TriBeCa, the lounge of this "gorgeous" bar/restaurant is an "open space" "nicely lit with candles" that's roomy enough for "big parties" yet "mellow" (and "empty") enough for a clandestine tryst; groupies hype its "beyond-good martinis" and luxe mood, "without the 'tude."

Ear Inn | 21 | 15 | 19 | $6 |
326 Spring St. (bet. Greenwich & Washington Sts.), 212-226-9060

■ "The antithesis of slick", this circa 1817 "granddaddy" of "old-time NY bars" in "way far West" SoHo allows "poets and plumbers to rub elbows" in a "rather messy" "historical" setting; seafarers in need of "divey relief" and "homemade" grub call it "a great place to have one more" and beg all to lend an ear – "it must be preserved!"

Edward Moran Bar & Grill | 16 | 13 | 13 | $6 |
World Financial Ctr., 250 Vesey St. (West Side Hwy.), 212-945-2255

■ After the closing bell, a "sea" of Wall Streeters crashes into this WFC "broker hangout", a grade-A "meat market" where "big crowds" of "hunky Merrill and Amex guys" and "Jersey babes" "get Schlitzed after a long day"; in summer it's a "Thursday night hot spot" with "indoor/outdoor" action and (anyone care?) a "nice view"; **N.B. closed at press time.**

Eight Mile Creek | 23 | 20 | 24 | $8 |
240 Mulberry St. (bet. Prince & Spring Sts.), 212-431-4635

■ Beneath the Little Italy Australian eatery of the same name lies this "warm" pub that boasts a "fantastic selection" of "real Aussie" grape and grain; staffed by a

Nightlife A | D | S | C

"friendly" crew of "transplanted" denizens, it's a natural for "conversation" and the occasional toast to Queen Vicky.

El Teddy's 20 | 19 | 17 | $8
219 W. Broadway (bet. Franklin & White Sts.), 212-941-7071
◪ Behind that "landmark" "neon sombrero" facade, this "quirky" "Tex-Mex" "TriBeCa standby" follows through with a "garish" "Gaudí-esque" interior and a "corporate" "singles" scene fueled by "mighty fine" margaritas; it's "popular" for "kitschy", "tequila-soaked" times, though some sense it's "not as hip as it used to be."

Fanelli's Cafe 19 | 16 | 18 | $6
94 Prince St. (Mercer St.), 212-226-9412
■ An "attitude-free find" in snoot central, this "older-than-earth" SoHo "stalwart" is a certified "drinker's" barroom that pours on the "surly" "charm"; "holdover" "art types" gather in the "dark" room to "pound beers", chow down "cheap bar food" and relive their greatest NEA grants.

55 Wall 21 | 21 | 21 | $9
Regent Wall Street Hotel, 55 Wall St. (bet. Hanover & William Sts.), 212-699-5555
■ Everyone's "all business" at this Financial District bar in a "gorgeous" "landmark" locale (once the NY Merchants Exchange) with classical flourishes and a "fabulous" seasonal patio offering commanding views of Wall Street; "priced for a bull market", it's the pride of every white-shoe "corporate tab" and puts the seal on many a deal.

FLOR DE SOL 25 | 24 | 22 | $7
361 Greenwich St. (bet. Franklin & Harrison Sts.), 212-334-6411
■ There's a "shortcut to Spain" via TriBeCa at this "sexy" tapas taberna, a place to "bat your eyelashes" over "fantastic sangria" and finger food delivered in "romantic" "close quarters" by a "flirtatious" staff; the "dark", "mysterious" interior is "medieval in a good way", with flamenco dancers on hand to keep things "lively."

Full Shilling ▽ 22 | 22 | 22 | $6
160 Pearl St. (bet. Pine & Wall Sts.), 212-422-3855
■ Other outposts of Gaeldom may claim to be the real deal, but this "friendly" entry was shipped piece by piece from Ireland onto Financial District sod; the staffers serve up grog like it's a "small-town pub" in County Cork, with the only incongruous touch being "lots of Wall Streeters" who keep it "packed after work"; N.B. closed on Saturday and Sunday.

Fun 20 | 22 | 16 | $8
130 Madison St. (bet. Market & Pike Sts.), 212-964-0303
■ Here's "something different" in a "hard-to-find" corner of Chinatown: a "sensory experience" for Gen Y where "video art" is projected onto "humongous screens" to the tune of "techy" music (hidden "camera monitors" also offer

68 www.zagat.com

Nightlife | A | D | S | C |

"sneak peeks" into the lavs); it's way "wicked" – picture a "rave" sans dancing – though now that it's "discovered", scenemakers sigh it was "fun . . . while it lasted."

Good World Bar & Grill | 24 | 19 | 19 | $7 |
3 Orchard St. (bet. Canal & Division Sts.), 212-925-9975
■ There's "never a dull moment" at this former barbershop on the Lower East Side that offers "yummy specialty drinks" and "odd Scandinavian cuisine" in a "funky", "low-key setting" that could "use a couch or ten" (the spartan "back patio area" absorbs any overflow); although its "weird location" can be "hard to find", the kewl "crowd makes it worth the trip."

GRACE | 23 | 22 | 21 | $8 |
114 Franklin St. (bet Church St. & W. B'way), 212-343-4200
■ "TriBeCa insiders" tout the "divine atmosphere" at this "handsome" watering hole that boasts an "extra-long mahogany bar" (one of the "longest in NY") topped by a "huge mirror" perfect for "checking out" its "eclectic", "very social" crowd; add "strong", "imaginative cocktails" that are "well worth the price" to the mix, and it's no wonder that many revere this "undiscovered gem" as a "role model" for its genre.

Grand Bar | 24 | 25 | 19 | $9 |
SoHo Grand Hotel, 310 W. Broadway, 2nd fl. (bet. Canal & Grand Sts.), 212-965-3000
■ "You can cut the chic with a knife" at this "très hip" bar on the second floor of the SoHo Grand, where lots of "fashionable" types – "actors, models", "waifs" and "famous" faces – strike a pose in "beautiful", wood-paneled digs that have been recently refurbished; despite all the "sunglasses" and "cell phones", fans insist you can actually meet "interesting people who can hold a conversation."

Harbour Lights | 22 | 20 | 18 | $8 |
South St. Seaport, Pier 17, 3rd fl. (bet. Fulton & South Sts.), 212-227-2800
■ "It's all about the view" at this patio-equipped South Street Seaport bar/eatery that overlooks the Brooklyn Bridge and is "one of the only decent places" in this tourist-clogged nabe; you can also expect a sizable "Wall Street" contingent, given the fairly hefty price tag; **N.B. closed at press time.**

Harry's at Hanover Square | 18 | 18 | 20 | $8 |
1 Hanover Sq. (bet. Pearl & Stone Sts.), 212-425-3412
■ "As much a part of Wall Street as the NYSE", this "classic" brokers' "hangout" is such a "men's club" you can almost "smell the testosterone" wafting through the clouds of "cigar smoke"; bulls tout the fine "selection of wines" and the "cool stock ticker", but bears surmise that regulars "never got the memo that the '80s are over."

www.zagat.com 69

Nightlife   A | D | S | C

IDLEWILD   20 | 25 | 17 | $7
145 E. Houston St. (bet. 1st & 2nd Aves.), 212-477-5005
■ "Frequent fliers" "sit in the airplane seats for the full effect" at this Lower East Side theme bar done up like a "late '60s Boeing 747" (right down to its tiny, "mile high club"–worthy bathrooms); some find it "more idle than wild" on weekdays, but passengers "cleared for departure" are always "flying high" here.

Iggy's Keltic Lounge   ▽ 19 | 16 | 21 | $6
132 Ludlow St. (bet. Rivington & Stanton Sts.), 212-529-2731
◪ "Great service" distinguishes this Irish Lower Eastsider improbably plopped down in the midst of the hip Ludlow Street scene, though diehards seeking a drink reminiscent of the Auld Sod say it's "not worth the trek to the edge of nowhere" to get one.

Independent, The   19 | 18 | 19 | $9
179 W. Broadway (bet. Leonard & Worth Sts.), 212-219-2010
◪ For boozers with bucks, the "fun bartenders" and "incredible bar food" are a "definite fit" at this TriBeCa duplex that's a sibling of the star-studded Bridgehamptonite; but the bargain-minded deride its "average", "overpriced" drinks, even though they can be sipped on a "wonderful" wooden deck that spills onto the sidewalk.

I Tre Merli   20 | 19 | 17 | $8
463 W. Broadway (bet. Houston & Prince Sts.), 212-254-8699
◪ "Sit at the bar with a drink and look beautiful" at this longtime SoHo restaurant/bar that might draw a slightly "stuck-up", "très Euro" crowd but still retains its romantic, "exposed-brick"-and-"candlelight" aura; those who find "something missing" finger the "attitude-driven" service.

Jeremy's Ale House   19 | 12 | 18 | $5
254 Front St. (Dover St.), 212-964-3537
■ Dirt-"cheap" suds come in "big" "Styrofoam cups" at this "garage"–turned–"beer hall" near the Brooklyn Bridge that's jammed with the "Wall Street exodus", "recessed jurors mulling the verdict" and early-birds chirping about its 8–10 AM happy hour; P.S. "don't wear a tie" or it may join the cast-off bra collection dangling from the ceiling.

John Street Bar & Grill   18 | 13 | 16 | $5
17 John St. (bet. B'way & Nassau St.), 212-349-3278
■ "You get what you pay for" at this "poor-man's choice" in the Financial District – "good weeknight specials" and a free hot buffet in a "dark, dingy" setting featuring "old sofas", dartboards and a pool table; still, for some "young Wall Street pros", the chance to "hear an entire Allman Brothers album" is "too good to pass up."

Nightlife | A | D | S | C |

Kaña | 22 | 15 | 15 | $7 |
324 Spring St. (bet. Greenwich & Washington Sts.), 212-343-8180
■ "Feel like you're in Bogota" at this West SoHo "hole-in-the-wall" where "authentic sangria" and "excellent tapas" thrill a "lively" crowd; "go late" to party to DJ'd Latin tunes, but beware of "butt pinchers" in the "too-crowded" room.

Kavehaz | 21 | 17 | 17 | $7 |
123 Mercer St. (bet. Spring & Prince Sts.), 212-343-0612
■ With a "display of local art" and nightly "jazz performed by unknowns", this "great SoHo oasis" is suitable for "snuggling", "snacking" and imbibing from the "good drink selection"; the trust fund–deprived go to "appear cultured on a first date without spending a lot of money" but warn the "acoustics may prevent conversation."

KNITTING FACTORY | 21 | 15 | 16 | $6 |
74 Leonard St. (bet. B'way & Church St.), 212-219-3006
■ "Home to the edgiest music in town", this TriBeCa complex of performance spaces is an "unbeatable" destination for "hip" NYers; though the established and "emerging artists" can be "strange" and the crowd can contain a few too many "boho wanna-bes", with "three floors of varied acts", there's "something for everyone."

KUSH | 23 | 25 | 19 | $8 |
183 Orchard St. (bet. E. Houston & Stanton Sts.), 212-677-7328
■ "Like being inside the *I Dream of Jeannie* bottle", this "sexy", Moroccan-themed Lower East Side lounge is an Eden for "romantics" with its "candlelit walls" and "peachy tobacco smells" wafting from hookahs; a "belly dancer" adds an "exotic" flavor to Sunday's "Middle Eastern night."

La Jumelle | 20 | 19 | 21 | $8 |
55 Grand St. (bet. W. B'way & Wooster St.), 212-941-9651
■ "Reasonably priced drinks" and "cheap, late-night" French fare turn up at this SoHo restaurant that's "always good" for a "quiet" dose of "Paris minus the attitude"; old tin advertising signs supply the atmosphere.

Lansky Lounge | 21 | 19 | 17 | $8 |
104 Norfolk St. (bet. Delancey & Rivington Sts.), 212-677-9489
◪ This "hip", onetime "speakeasy" on the Lower East Side has expanded its restaurant space by annexing a chunk of Ratner's, but you still must maneuver a "subterranean labyrinth" to enter (though a newly added sign takes some of the mystery away); foes say it's more like "crashing a bar mitzvah" than a "Jewish gangster hideout."

Laparue | ▽ 22 | 19 | 17 | $9 |
345 Greenwich St. (bet. Harrison & Jay Sts.), 212-625-9820
■ "Loft-like looks" "make you feel like you're at a private party" full of "minimalist hip"-sters at this TriBeCa lounge

Nightlife | A | D | S | C |

that's a "great place to people-watch" while nibbling tapas (though some say "it's kind of weak weeknights"); whenever you come, "remember to touch the dog", the canine statue near the door; **N.B. closed at press time.**

Le Zinc | 22 | 21 | 20 | $8 |
139 Duane St. (bet. Church St. & W. B'way), 212-513-0001
■ The owners of TriBeCa's ultra-civilized Chanterelle let their hair down at this "relaxed" satellite that "has promise" as an "after-hours scene", since it serves both food and drink till the wee hours; though the furnishings are a bit "stark" and the small bar area can get "overcrowded" at prime times, night owls hoot it's "fine and dandy" later on.

Liquor Store Bar ⇗ | 21 | 15 | 20 | $6 |
235 W. Broadway (White St.), 212-226-7121
■ The "liquor store facade" remains from an earlier incarnation, but inside this "old, run-down" bar you'll encounter one of "TriBeCa's friendliest" crowds; both couch potatoes and their pooches are welcome, and during clement weather, it's hard to "walk by without stopping for a drink" at one of the sidewalk tables.

Living Room ⇗ | 19 | 15 | 18 | $6 |
84 Stanton St. (Allen St.), 212-533-7235
■ "Up-and-coming folk rockers" and other "appealing" acoustic performers hone their chops at this "artsy" Lower East Side "corner bar" that's a "casual, friendly hangout" for everyone from "body-pierced locals" to "fortysomethings who wish they were kids" again; though bigger than some living rooms, it's still "too damn small" for claustrophobes.

Local 138 | 20 | 16 | 20 | $6 |
138 Ludlow St. (bet. Rivington & Stanton Sts.), 212-477-0280
■ "Bartenders with [Irish] accents" dispense the suds at this Lower East Side version of "Dublin on the Hudson", judged one of the "coziest bars" around; insiders arrive early to snag the snugs, two "semi-private" booths facing the street, where "passersby can watch you get drunk."

Lolita | – | – | – | I |
266 Broome St. (Allen St.), 212-966-7223
No Nabokovian touches are apparent at this new Lower East Side lounge that works on the anti-fashion principle, with an ironic go-to-hell attitude that matches the mood of the crowd; the music's eclectic, and as for the decor, picture a garage sale where nothing's been sold yet.

L'Orange Bleue | 20 | 20 | 19 | $8 |
430 Broome St. (Crosby St.), 212-226-4999
■ When its "multiculti crowd" of "world travelers" and local "bohemians" descends on this SoHo French-Moroccan, there can be "more air kissing than on Bastille Day", probably because the "bar area is too small" for more

Nightlife A D S C

elaborate expressions of affection; things take a more exotic turn Mondays, when the staff "pushes the tables aside" to give the belly dancer some room.

Lotus Cafe 23 | 22 | 17 | M
35 Clinton St. (Stanton St.), 212-253-1144
■ "Sit, chill and watch the Lower East Sideness" of it all at this Clinton Street coffeehouse that seems "more of a bar", since they roll up the food before dinner and concentrate on the libations thereafter; "cozy" enough on a quiet night, it can get too "sardine can–ish" on weekends.

Lucky Strike 19 | 17 | 17 | $7
59 Grand St. (bet. W. B'way & Wooster St.), 212-941-0479
◪ "Still packing 'em in after a decade", this eternally "reliable" SoHo brasserie is "always happening", though "never *too* hip"; sure, it's "a little worn", "loud" and "smoky", but it does feature "yummy martinis", a "consistently good crowd" and enough magnetism that if "you go for a beer, you stay for the night."

Ludlow Bar 18 | 13 | 17 | $6
165 Ludlow St. (bet. E. Houston & Stanton Sts.), 212-353-0536
◪ Locals "show up incoherent and stay incoherent" at this "dark" Lower East Side "underground lair" where you shouldn't "expect to meet a normal person", so you better be in the mood for some "diverse" characters; sure, the "ceiling is low" and it's "not comfortable" (almost "claustrophobic"), but the "music's good" and the bartenders are "dependable."

Luna Lounge ⌀ 19 | 16 | 18 | $6
171 Ludlow St. (bet. E. Houston & Stanton Sts.), 212-260-2323
■ While it may be "too dark" and looks as if they "haven't bought the decorations yet", this "artsy" Lower East Side bar radiates "hippie cool"; its "mixed crowd" touts the "amazing jukebox", "best foosball table in NY" and "up-and-coming bands" wailing in the back room.

Lush 21 | 22 | 19 | $8
110 Duane St. (bet. B'way & Church St.), 212-766-1275
◪ Glide into this "relaxed" TriBeCa lounge with a "perfect pickup atmosphere" reminiscent of a "Dartmouth and Sarah Lawrence after-party"; among its other assets are "tilted mirrors made for perfect people-watching" and a "cool oval room in back", but "be careful you don't walk right past the place", as it's in "no-man's land."

M & R Bar 21 | 18 | 19 | $7
264 Elizabeth St. (bet. Houston & Prince Sts.), 212-226-0559
■ Bop "back to the beatnik period" at this "funky" Little Italy bistro/bar, a "'50s-style cocktail lounge" (and Marion's Continental sib) that draws an "unpretentious", "good-time" clientele that supplies the "hip undercurrent"; granted,

Nightlife   A | D | S | C

the quarters are "very tight", so every-nighters either "go early" or slip "out back" to its "comfortable" garden during clement weather.

Mare Chiaro   ▽ 23 | 23 | 18 | $5
176½ Mulberry St. (bet. Broome & Grand Sts.), 212-226-9345
■ "Always and forever the real thing", this Little Italy "find" has been out there since 1908 but gained more recent renown when it was immortalized on celluloid in *Donnie Brasco*; though the "drink selection stinks", the "place is so cool" that even the most jaded Downtowners manage to have "tons of fun" here.

Max Fish   18 | 16 | 16 | $6
178 Ludlow St. (bet. E. Houston & Stanton Sts.), 212-529-3959
◪ "The bar that began it all for the Lower East Side", this "artsy" "stalwart" still provides a "chill atmosphere", the "best pinball" and "cool art" (rotated monthly); unless you drink like a fish, its "garish", "coffee shop"–style lighting might "push you over the edge", yet that doesn't seem to faze the "grungy" "young crowd, aspiring to poverty."

Mehanata 416 B.C.   – | – | – | M
416 Broadway (Canal St.), 212-625-0981
"Boozy fun in many languages" is in abundant supply at this tiny "Eastern European hot spot", the city's only Bulgarian bar/eatery, teetering on the border of SoHo and TriBeCa; when the weekend DJ spins gypsy rhythms, some say it "feels like a bar mitzvah", and the selection of Belgian wines makes the cultural confusion complete.

MEOW MIX   16 | 11 | 15 | $5
269 E. Houston St. (Suffolk St.), 212-254-0688
◪ "Tattooed lesbians" with "an edge" and the "women who love them" purr that this Lower East Side "dive bar" is a "hip change of pace" and the most "reliable" of the genre; sure, it's kind of "junky" and "rough around the edges", but "hot go-go girls" and a fun downstairs space – when it's open – supply the "kicks" here.

Mercantile Grill   ▽ 21 | 19 | 19 | $6
126 Pearl St. (bet. Hanover Sq. & Wall St.), 212-482-1221
■ Don't let the name fool you: the Wall Street crew leaves commerce behind at this "noisy, bustling" bar/eatery where "friendly service", "reasonable prices" and "great music" make for a rollicking setup to "catch up" on office gossip.

Merc Bar   21 | 20 | 17 | $8
151 Mercer St. (bet. Houston & Prince Sts.), 212-966-2727
■ "Not too yuppie, not too chic, not too stuffy", this longtime "SoHo staple" is "just right" for "chill" cocktails in a rustic setting embellished with "beautiful wood and leather motifs"; scenesters yawn it's "past its prime" and "starting to feel old", but the majority insists this "still hot" spot that's "always packed" "hasn't changed" one bit.

Nightlife   A | D | S | C

Mercer Bar   23 | 22 | 19 | $9
Mercer Hotel, 99 Prince St. (Mercer St.), 212-966-5454
■ "Still going strong", this "experience in SoHo chic" set in the Mercer Hotel remains an "ultrahip" nexus when the mood strikes to "stand around and admire" "pretty people"; sure, the "all-about-image" scene can be "heavy on the 'tude" and there's "not enough seating", yet "if you want to be seen and don't have anything to say", look no further.

Mercury Lounge   19 | 15 | 17 | $6
217 E. Houston St. (bet. Essex & Ludlow Sts.), 212-260-4700
■ "Trust the bookers" at this "crowded" Lower East Side "band bar" showcasing "lineups that almost never miss" ("you may see the next Lenny Kravitz here"); though it's usually "standing room only" and the overall look may be "generic", you "go for the music, not the atmosphere."

Mexican Radio   20 | 18 | 19 | $7
19 Cleveland Pl. (bet. Kenmare & Spring Sts.), 212-343-0140
■ Thirty brands of tequila and a swell variety of "Mexican beer on tap" make this Little Italy bar/cantina a bona fide destination for south-of-the-border buffs bent on "letting the good times roll, baby"; aesthetes aver its new, bi-level location "has no charm", but expansive types say it's certainly more "spacious" than its predecessor and just as "great" a "hangout."

Milady's   17 | 11 | 17 | $6
162 Prince St. (Thompson St.), 212-226-9340
■ "Regular people" swear there's still some "sanity in SoHo" at this "straightforward" saloon that's been a "dive" "holdout" on the scene since the 1920s; snobs sneer it's "worthy of patronage only if nearby", but average Joes find it just plain "refreshing" compared with "all the attitude" swirling around it.

Milano's Bar ⌿   ▽ 17 | 15 | 18 | $5
51 E. Houston St. (bet. Mott & Mulberry Sts.), 212-226-8844
■ "Workmen, professional drunks and writers" congregate at this "awesome" NoLita venue that's ready on the spot "if you need a drink at noon", with plenty of "Sinatra" on the jukebox to keep you company; when it comes to "authentic" "dive" atmosphere, it's "one of the last" of its kind.

MILK AND HONEY   25 | 23 | 27 | $7
134 Eldridge St. (bet. Broome & Delancey Sts.), unlisted phone
■ This "must-be-kept secret" on the Lower East Side has a pronounced "speakeasy" feel, since there's "no sign" and you must "call first" to get in (after obtaining the secret phone number from a regular); speed dialers with "insider knowledge" say their "lips are sealed" – "I could tell you, but then I'd have to kill you" – though they're willing to shout about its superb service, voted tops in town in the *NYC Nightlife Survey*.

www.zagat.com

Nightlife   A | D | S | C

Mint   – | – | – | E
225 E. Houston St. (Essex St.), 212-475-3200
Hoping to reenergize what was formerly known as Chaos, this new incarnation of the Lower East Side dance club has a name befitting its former bank building space, and prices to match; inside, you can expect the same hot Gucci-clad crowd as before, and the same wanna-bes lined up around the corner outside; N.B. open Friday–Sunday only.

Mooza   – | – | – | M
191 Orchard St. (bet. Houston & Stanton Sts.), 212-982-4770
New Lower East Side bar/bistro with decor that's a charming mishmash of crimson-flocked wallpaper, leopard-skin upholstery, mosaic tiles and some modern artwork thrown in for good measure; it all serves as a prelude to a smashing back garden/patio that's right up there in the see-it-to-believe-it pantheon; pounce on this one.

Motor City Bar ⌀   21 | 21 | 19 | $5
127 Ludlow St. (bet. Delancey & Rivington Sts.), 212-358-1595
■ Start your engines, "let off steam" or "motor through the night" at this Detroit-themed Lower East Side "dive" where DJs spin "kick-ass" "retro rock and punk"; a couple of "real bikers scattered here and there" add authenticity to the "Harley's-R-Us" decor, while faux hot-rodders rev up with one of their 'oil-change shots.'

Ñ ⌀   23 | 20 | 19 | $7
33 Crosby St. (bet. Broome & Grand Sts.), 212-219-8856
■ "If it were four times its size", this "teeny little" SoHo tapas bar "would still be packed" with "impenetrable crowds", thanks to its "sexy vibe", "fab tapas and sangria" and "awesome" Wednesday-night flamenco; so until the "serious lack of seating" problem is solved, either "get there early" or "come alone."

Naked Lunch   19 | 16 | 16 | $7
17 Thompson St. (Grand St.), 212-343-0828
◪ A "DJ who knows how to move the crowd" makes the twinkle-toed wish this SoHo bar was "bigger", since there's "never enough space" for "drunken dancing" here; regulars promise it's "more fun than it looks from the outside", but outsiders deride the "lame bouncers" who "keep you on line for an eternity" and "totally ruin the beginning of the night."

Nancy Whiskey   ▽ 16 | 10 | 19 | $5
1 Lispenard St. (W. B'way), 212-226-9943
■ One of the first taprooms to set up hops in the nabe, this "TriBeCa pioneer" might be the "ultimate dive", but it compensates with excellent "bang for the buck", including some of the "cheapest pitchers" in town; folks looking to get lost luxuriate in its middle-of-nowhere, "upstate feel."

Nightlife A | D | S | C

No Moore 19 | 15 | 18 | $6
234 W. Broadway (N. Moore St.), 212-925-2595
■ "Groovy in its simplicity", this "plain" but "spacious" TriBeCan spreads out three bars over two levels and draws a crowd that runs the gamut from "suits" to "Miramax employees"; though it no longer offers live entertainment, the drinks are still "semi-cheap" and it's "not inhibiting, unlike many" of its neighbors.

NVBar/289 Lounge 20 | 21 | 16 | $8
289 Spring St. (Hudson St.), 212-929-6868
◪ "Hit the floor" and "dance your butt off" at this "best of both worlds" SoHo nightclub where there's "room enough to groove" either in its downstairs danceteria or upstairs lounge; though the "cover is steep" and it can be "overrun" by "cross-bridge folks", most find it a "solid" "blast on Saturday nights" – "if you can get in."

Obeca Li 21 | 23 | 18 | $9
62 Thomas St. (bet. Church St. & W. B'way), 212-393-9887
■ The "enormous", "loft"-like interior of this "upscale", multilevel Japanese bar/eatery soothes "sophisticated" folk seeking "airy", "très chic" imbibing; though some say this TriBeCan seems to be "always empty", maybe that's because insiders "get a private room and have some fun", as it's "fantastic for parties."

Odeon 22 | 20 | 20 | $8
145 W. Broadway (bet. Duane & Thomas Sts.), 212-233-0507
■ A "bar you can trust", this ever-"busy" "TriBeCa evergreen" (since 1980) is a "good place to be an adult", given lighting so flattering "you could not sleep for a week and still look great"; no surprise, there can be waits to get in, so hepcats turn up later in the evening.

Onieal's Grand Street 21 | 21 | 20 | $8
174 Grand St. (bet. Centre & Mulberry Sts.), 212-941-9119
◪ A "former speakeasy" reputedly patronized by Teddy Roosevelt, this "historic" spot on the border of Little Italy is today an "elegant oasis" most notable for its "cushy" couches and very low lighting; "generous bartenders" help compensate for the somewhat "overpriced" pours.

Orange Bear 13 | 10 | 15 | $5
47 Murray St. (bet. Church St. & W. B'way), 212-566-3705
◪ Ok, there's "no atmosphere whatsoever" at this City Hall–area "pit" that might "need a mop" but wipes out the competition by offering "live original music" from either "up-and-coming" bands or "untalented musicians with tenacity"; understandably, the drinks are "quite cheap."

Orchard Bar 20 | 18 | 18 | $7
200 Orchard St. (bet. Houston & Stanton Sts.), 212-673-5350
■ It helps to be "skinny" "'cause that's the only way you'll fit" into this "narrow" lounge, one of the first "hipster" lairs

www.zagat.com 77

Nightlife   A | D | S | C

on the Lower East Side; it's "hard to find" (no sign), but once inside, its half-filled aquariums, potted plants and "crazy lighting" have such a "calming" effect that you might be tempted to venture to the back for a little "PDA."

Paris Cafe ▽ 17 | 16 | 16 | $6
119 South St. (Peck Slip), 212-240-9797
◪ Everyone from Thomas Edison to Teddy Roosevelt has patronized this circa 1873 South Street Seaport "hideaway", although today you can expect "locals only" propping up its original hand-carved bar; some landlubbers sniff it's "too close to the fish market", yet satisfied seafarers say you can't beat the "cheap-beer"-and-fresh-oysters combo.

Peasant 23 | 22 | 20 | $8
194 Elizabeth St. (bet. Prince & Spring Sts.), 212-965-9511
■ Save the serious drinking until after you've tackled the "complicated", foreign-language menu at this NoLita "gem" featuring a long bar that's plenty "comfy" whether you're dining or not; though the acoustics in this "concrete"-lined space used to draw brickbats, there's no need to "scream" anymore – they've mercifully "added soundproofing."

Pig N Whistle 14 | 13 | 16 | $6
365 Greenwich St. (bet. Franklin & Harrison Sts.), 212-941-1771
■ This "quintessential Irish pub" in TriBeCa might be a "standard", "no-frills" affair, yet can be amusing, since it's "filled with characters" and staffed by "salty" servers who all appear to have "come from Ireland"; folks find it "handy" when in the mood for an "honest beer", but ultimately "nothing special."

Pink Pony Cafe ⊭ 21 | 15 | 18 | $5
176 Ludlow St. (bet. E. Houston & Stanton Sts.), 212-253-1922
■ "You can read or work all day, like in a European cafe", at this "grungy" Lower East Side coffeehouse "bohemia" where "artist/poet/musician types" migrate for a java jolt; sure, it's a "bit of a dump" and "they allow smoking" (hence the "stale air"), but "cute counter help" and a "great bulletin board" kind of compensate.

PRAVDA 22 | 23 | 18 | $9
281 Lafayette St. (bet. Houston & Prince Sts.), 212-226-4944
■ "In vodka, pravda", and the truth is, this subterranean SoHocialist lounge is as "stylish" as ever, even if the "hype has died down"; expect an "always crowded but tolerable" scene perfumed with "thick clouds of smoke" and a whiff of "arrogance" ("practice your poses in advance"), yet in return there are some mighty "amazing martinis" and snacks served in "ultrachic" digs.

PUCK FAIR 20 | 19 | 20 | $6
298 Lafayette St. (bet. Houston & Prince Sts.), 212-431-1200
■ "Heavenly suds drawn from chilled taps" make the mood "magical" at this "fresh Irish face" in SoHo, a tri-level affair

Nightlife A | D | S | C

that manages to be both "big and cozy at the same time"; fans "love the snugs" and the encyclopedic variety of beers (though "Guinness rules"), while its central location is a "nice, convenient" stop "after getting laid off from your dot-com."

Puffy's Tavern 16 | 12 | 17 | $5
81 Hudson St. (Harrison St.), 212-766-9159
■ Long "before the models and rocks stars moved in" to "trendy Tribecaland", there was this "soulful hole" that's been dispensing "quick" pops in a "seedy" setting since 1945; though too "down and out" for arrivistes, most breathe "thank God" there's "no Puffy, no Jennifer" and "no scene."

Raccoon Lodge 13 | 10 | 15 | $5
59 Warren St. (W. B'way), 212-766-9656
◪ This Financial District "rock-'em, sock-'em dive bar is renowned for its "party"-hearty atmosphere, "skid-row" decor and "stale beer smell"; no surprise, "you don't go for beautiful people", but rather for "hilarious people-watching" of the "biker" and "frat boy" variety.

Raoul's 24 | 21 | 21 | $9
180 Prince St. (bet. Sullivan & Thompson Sts.), 212-966-3518
■ "Still great after all these years" – 27, to be exact – this French bistro "staple" is "sexy", cozy and hip all at the same time", yet "completely lacks SoHo pretense"; no surprise, it works both as an "understated pickup scene" and as a "place to rub elbows with the Hollywood set."

Recess 21 | 18 | 18 | $7
310 Spring St. (bet. Greenwich & Renwick Sts.), 646-590-6050
■ "Out of the way" in a "sketchy area", this "laid-back" SoHo lounge still gets "packed" with a "young crowd" as well as "spillovers and rejects from Sway" across the street; credit the "super staff" for its popularity, not to mention its "board games", free snacks and "comfortable couches."

Red Bench 22 | 18 | 19 | $7
107 Sullivan St. (bet. Prince & Spring Sts.), 212-274-9120
◪ For "a perfect retreat while waiting for a table at Blue Ribbon Sushi", nip into this "adorable" SoHo "hideaway"; granted, it's so "tiny" and "dark" that it might be "tough to maneuver" once inside, but it's "not well known", so you'll "never get caught" if an illicit rendezvous is on the agenda.

Remy Lounge 17 | 17 | 15 | $7
104 Greenwich St. (bet. Carlisle & Rector Sts.), 212-267-4646
◪ "Fantastic" hip-hop and salsa has bon-bons shaking so furiously at this "lively" double-decker TriBeCa "meat market" that it puts the Latin in Manhattan for the "suit-and-tie" set; yet in spite of the "pounding" beats and "endless energy", picky partiers pronounce the scene "a bit stale";
N.B. closed at press time.

www.zagat.com

Nightlife A | D | S | C

Rialto   20 | 19 | 17 | $8
265 Elizabeth St. (bet. Houston & Prince Sts.), 212-334-7900
◪ Maybe not much is new at this Rialto, a garden-equipped Little Italy lounge/eatery that might be "more restaurant than bar" but is still "romantic" enough to make it a fine "first date spot"; spoilers find "nothing to write home about", save the "inattentive service."

Rivertown Lounge   20 | 17 | 19 | $6
187 Orchard St. (bet. E. Houston & Stanton Sts.), 212-388-1288
◼ "Tons of couches", "cool artwork" and a "nice pool table" set the "laid-back" scene at this Lower East Side lounge that might not enjoy the rep of the neighboring Orchard Bar, yet still has adherents sticking to it; even if your posse consists of "eight guys and no girls", you'll feel "welcome" here.

RM   21 | 17 | 18 | $8
(fka Rubber Monkey)
279 Church St. (White St.), 212-625-8220
◼ One of the "many upstarts jumping into TriBeCa", this new club distinguishes itself with a "dope space" featuring "three different atmospheres": a "small" bar area, a "totally fun" cabaret room and a "downstairs dance floor with pumping music", all adorned with eclectic, slightly "off-color" artwork; maybe it "needs promotion", since it's "not so crowded", but that suits "cool Downtown" claustrophobes just fine.

Room, The ⌀   22 | 21 | 20 | $7
144 Sullivan St. (bet. Houston & Prince Sts.), 212-477-2102
◼ Since it's so "small", this "sultry", "candlelit" SoHo bar is something of a chameleon: it can be "comfy" and "mellow" or way "too crowded", depending on the hour; the booze lineup is more predictable – "only wine and beer" – though the "good selection" keeps the crowds content.

Sapphire Lounge   15 | 13 | 14 | $7
249 Eldridge St. (bet. E. Houston & Stanton Sts.), 212-777-5153
◪ For a "crazy evening" of "anonymous", "sweaty dancing" and "groping", "old-school hip-hop" fans descend on this tiny Lower East Side club where the "music and the prices are right"; perfectionists say it "needs a makeover badly", as the name makes you "expect more creativity inside."

Savoy   24 | 24 | 22 | $9
70 Prince St. (Crosby St.), 212-219-8570
◼ "NY's most sophisticated drinking spot" just might be this "oh-so-romantic" lounge tucked above a Mediterranean "sleeper" restaurant in SoHo; canoodlers "linger" beside

Nightlife | A | D | S | C |

the "nice fireplace" and breathe it's a surefire way to "win your lady's heart" – provided your honeybun doesn't mind a setting that's "*really* small."

Screening Room 22 | 21 | 20 | $8
54 Varick St. (Laight St.), 212-334-2100
■ "Eat, drink and see a movie" at this "civilized", one-of-a-kind TriBeCan that might be "out of the way" but has "first date" written all over it; though eavesdroppers are amused to "overhear film buffs trying to outdo each other", cynical cineasts wonder "how many times can you see *Breakfast at Tiffany's*?"

Shine 20 | 18 | 16 | $8
285 W. Broadway (Canal St.), 212-941-0900
◪ For the ultimate "bang for the buck", try this TriBeCa club/performance space where young nighthawks "never know what to expect", given a menu of everything from cabaret to "wild" circus-style entertainment to acts heavy on the "shock factor"; non-observers hit the "traffic zone" of a dance floor or hang in the lounge area, but always call ahead, since the programming changes each night.

SLIPPER ROOM 19 | 20 | 17 | $7
167 Orchard St. (Stanton St.), 212-253-7246
■ Cabaret gets the Lower East Side treatment at this Fellini-esque lounge where the "peculiar entertainment" includes everything from "drag queens" and "drag kings" to "burlesque" and beyond; the "changing crowd" of "freak show" followers – everyone from "bachelorettes" to folks with more "questionable sexual preferences" – reports it's "cool", "crowded" and deliciously "bizarre."

S.O.B.'s 21 | 18 | 17 | $8
204 Varick St. (W. Houston St.), 212-243-4940
■ "Be in the mood for craziness" at this "hot, hot, hot" Latin dance club in SoHo, where folks of "all ages" and "all colors" who "know how to party" show up "rarin' to go"; though the decor veers toward "cheesy" and the "cover can be steep", the "real island" music is such "infectious", "shameless fun" that it's virtually impossible to "stay seated."

SouthWest NY 20 | 20 | 18 | $8
2 World Financial Ctr. (bet. Liberty & Vesey Sts.), 212-945-0528
■ "Wall Street types" keep this "classy" cantina in the World Financial Center "jam-packed", especially at "Thursday night's meat market" and in "warm weather", when outdoor seats with marina views are the way to go; year-round, you can expect "knockout margaritas", though the pricing leaves tightwads gasping "ouch"; **N.B. closed at press time.**

www.zagat.com

Nightlife A | D | S | C

Sporting Club 19 | 16 | 15 | $6
99 Hudson St. (bet. Franklin & Leonard Sts.), 212-219-0900
■ "Watch a game and celebrate a win" at this TriBeCa "large-screen" nexus where "real sports fans" "get a table and stay all spring"; hard-core "jocks" applaud it "hands down" as "the best in NY", noting that 'scoring' here has multiple meanings, given the opportunities via "girls, games and pool."

Spring Lounge 20 | 15 | 20 | $6
48 Spring St. (Mulberry St.), 212-965-1774
■ It's "always crowded" at this "low-key", longtime NoLita "dive" that's been around under different names since the '20s and is unofficially known as the 'Shark Bar', what with all the stuffed fish decorating the walls; disgruntled locals lament that this "feels-like-home" spot is lately being "overrun by Uptown bankers wanting to feel Downtown."

Sugar 23 | 21 | 20 | $9
311 Church St. (bet. Lispenard & Walker Sts.), 212-431-8642
■ "TriBeCa's getting better" following the arrival of this "trendy" new bar/lounge that "leaves a sweet taste in the mouth" thanks to smart decor that's an unlikely blend of Danish Modern and "African artifacts"; still, aesthetes advise you "stay upstairs", as the basement dance floor might be a bit too reminiscent of "your parent's rec room."

Sway 22 | 21 | 17 | $9
305 Spring St. (bet. Greenwich & Hudson Sts.), 212-620-5220
◪ "Part Marrakech, part Paris", this SoHo lounge is a late-late, "laid-back" lair where "scenesters" get "comfy" and "let it all hang out"; insiders wink "don't be fooled by the [McGovern's] sign" outside, though the 'out' crowd is outraged by all the "abuse and attitude" at the "tough door."

Sweet & Vicious ⊅ 20 | 19 | 17 | $7
5 Spring St. (bet. Bowery & Elizabeth St.), 212-334-7915
■ "Forget the silly name" – this "relaxed" Turkish bar in NoLita is as "unpretentious" as can be, with a "spunky crowd" unwinding in digs that are "long", "spacious" and "more sweet than vicious"; adding to the feeling of "cool chill" is a very hot "outside space in the back."

Swim 21 | 19 | 17 | $7
146 Orchard St. (bet. Rivington & Stanton Sts.), 212-673-0799
■ "Donners of black" float by this "very cool" Lower East Side bar for its "hip" vibe and "awesome DJ"; although the upstairs sushi bar is no more, making for a smaller, more "narrow" scene, its "long happy hour" picks up the slack.

82 www.zagat.com

Nightlife | A | D | S | C |

Sx 137 | – | – | – | E |
137 Essex St. (bet. Rivington & Stanton Sts.), 212-674-6931
Park Avenue South lands on Essex Street at this ultrasleek new bar/restaurant that relies on lacquered plywood, polished stainless steel and a zillion votive candles for its effects (local artists' work is showcased in the hallways as an afterthought); so far, the crowd seems comprised of laid-back, laid-off dot-commers economizing by having cocktails instead of wine.

Thom's Bar | – | – | – | E |
60 Thompson Hotel, 60 Thompson St. (bet. Broome & Spring Sts.), 212-219-2000
Yet another entry in the burgeoning boutique hotel bar scene, this SoHo venue stands apart from the crowd only because it's located on one of the least-trafficked streets in the neighborhood; otherwise, it's a standard-issue hipster lounge populated by a make-it-happen crowd waiting for something to happen.

357 | ▽ 22 | 20 | 19 | $9 |
357 W. Broadway (bet. Broome & Grand Sts.), 212-965-1491
◼ Few night-crawlers are hep to this "expensive", smallish SoHo lounge that evokes mixed emotions: enthusiasts say it "tries hard" and "holds its own" against the competition, but crybabies moan the "doormen should cool down – it's not that exclusive."

TJA! | 22 | 22 | 17 | $9 |
301 Church St. (Walker St.), 212-226-8900
◼ "Beautiful creatures abound" at this swell new TriBeCa bar/eatery where an "eclectic" crowd of "Euro" expats and "amazing models" tries its damnedest not to be upstaged by the "unbelievably hot waitresses"; while the "Zen"-meets-"Ikea" decor is "appealing", it's the restaurant's "Scandin-asian" fusion menu (one part Japanese, one part Swedish) that's the conversation starter here.

Toad Hall | 19 | 16 | 19 | $6 |
57 Grand St. (bet. W. B'way & Wooster St.), 212-431-8145
◼ Hopped-up fans "dig the name" of this "low-key" SoHo watering hole that supplies "convivial" times despite a "dingy, crowded" setting that's out of sync with its tony neighbors; so long as you lower your expectations, its "no-attitude" attitude and "fun billiards" scene just might "put the wind in your willows."

Tonic ⌐ | 21 | 17 | 18 | $7 |
107 Norfolk St. (bet. Delancey & Rivington Sts.), 212-358-7501
◼ "Experimental, cutting-edge acts" fill out the "solid", eclectic musical roster at this avant-garde Lower Eastsider,

Nightlife | A | D | S | C |

while in the basement (a former winery), you can "hang out in old kosher wine casks" converted into seating and ponder "spoken-word" performers; those who find things not so bracing moan about the "weak drinks" and "high covers" to get in.

TORCH | 23 | 24 | 19 | $9 |
137 Ludlow St. (bet. Rivington & Stanton Sts.), 212-228-5151
■ "Behind its beautiful doors", this "sultry" "throwback to the '40s" is "very grown-up for the Lower East Side", featuring "sexy cocktails" and "Sinatra"-esque "torch singers"; locals lament the "intellectual" "Yale-y" types who occasionally turn up, but its "hipster" contingent "loves the concept" and rates it one of the "hottest places to take a date" around.

Tribeca Blues | ▽ | 19 | 18 | 21 | $7 |
16 Warren St. (bet. B'way & Church St.), 212-766-1070
◪ Ok, there's "no atmosphere" at this "standard" issue roadhouse/blues club that snobs snipe is "not good enough for TriBeCa", but fans find its brick-walled, sofa-strewn digs "cozy", the acts appealing and the prices right; icing the cake is some mighty tasty "homemade, happy-hour" grub.

Tribeca Grill | 23 | 22 | 22 | $9 |
375 Greenwich St. (Franklin St.), 212-941-3900
■ "Famous owners" Robert De Niro and Drew Nieporent are the minds behind this "fabuloso" TriBeCa bar/restaurant, a "trusty spot" that's "spacious", "airy" and home to both a "nice wine list" and "one of the best martinis in town"; though trendoids say this 11-year-old has morphed into a "waiting room for Nobu", there's concurrence that its "easygoing" charm is nothing less than "spectacular."

Tribeca Tavern | 21 | 19 | 21 | $6 |
247 W. Broadway (bet. Beach & Walker Sts.), 212-941-7671
■ For a "nontrendy spot in trendy TriBeCa", slummers slither by this "comfortable" if funky saloon that's "way cooler than its uppity neighbors", given its absolute absense of attitude; the "huge space" has the added benefit of two entrances – one on West Broadway, the other on Sixth Avenue – just right for quick getaways.

205 Club ⌀ | ▽ | 15 | 10 | 14 | $6 |
205 Chrystie St. (Stanton St.), 212-473-5816
◪ Thanks to a stellar stable of DJs, you can count on "great" grooves at this Lower East Side hip-hop club that's "packed" with hearty partiers, even though there's barely enough "room to dance or breathe"; set in a former bodega, what it lacks in decor is made up for with high energy; N.B. open Thursday–Saturday only.

Nightlife   A D S C

203 Spring St.   21 | 19 | 16 | $8
203 Spring St. (Sullivan St.), 212-334-3855
■ "Despite having no [official] name", this SoHo venue is "no longer a secret" but rather is a magnet for enough runway-ready types that it "should be called Models, Inc."; "dark and sexy" with a "super-comfortable" back lounge, it's just the ticket "for a relaxing evening with friends" – provided you're willing to cough up the cash on weekends for an "expensive" bottle of booze to secure a table.

Velvet Restaurant & Lounge   20 | 19 | 18 | $8
223 Mulberry St. (bet. Prince & Spring Sts.), 212-965-0439
■ "Wonderfully romantic", this "dark and sexy" bar/eatery in NoLita is a "safe bet" for some "very chill" canoodling, especially upstairs in the "comfy", "classy" lounge, where folks through with love opt instead for a game of chess or backgammon; there is some debate over its popularity: "nobody there" vs. "needs a bouncer for crowd control."

Veruka   19 | 18 | 16 | $9
525 Broome St. (bet. 6th Ave. & Thompson St.), 212-625-1717
◪ "Skinny", "pretty people" still mingle with "cliquey" "men in black" beyond the velvet ropes of this bi-level SoHo lounge, but it's "not impossible to get in" nowadays, as it's "not the scene it used to be"; though "Derek Jeter" might be long gone, it "still can be fun"; N.B. a recent redo is not yet reflected in its decor rating.

Vig Bar   20 | 19 | 19 | $7
12 Spring St. (Elizabeth St.), 212-625-0011
◪ "Hip, but not too hip", this NoLita entry offers a "cool" enough vibe for you to "get quietly smashed without anybody noticing" – provided you're in its "awesome" back room, the "only way to go" here; up front, gird yourself for a "smoky" "sardine can" scene, especially on "Thursdays."

Vinyl ⊘   24 | 16 | 17 | $7
6 Hubert St. (bet. Greenwich & Hudson Sts.), 212-343-1379
■ "Be prepared to sweat" at this "hard-core" TriBeCa danceteria that provides "no decor", "no alcohol" and "no attitude"; instead, it's the "excellent energy" that keeps its patchwork quilt of "ethnic straights, hip white kids and Chelsea boys" occupied – that is, when they're not applauding DJ Danny Tenaglia's Friday night 'Be Yourself' party or the legendary Sunday afternoon 'Body & Soul' extravaganza.

Void   21 | 21 | 17 | $7
16 Mercer St. (Howard St.), 212-941-6492
■ A "dark", "film noir–ish" atmosphere draws "Downtown" denizens to this relatively "low-profile" SoHo multimedia

Nightlife A D S C

bar/lounge that's just the ticket when you're in a "vanish-into-the-night" state of mind; complimentary online access, "cool" experimental flicks and "loud" ambient sounds make this "mix of art and drinks" a distractingly "interesting experience" for most.

Walker's   21 | 17 | 19 | $6
16 N. Moore St. (Varick St.), 212-941-0142
■ This "down-to-earth bar in not very down-to-earth" TriBeCa is an out-and-out "miracle": an "unpretentious", "grab-a-beer-and-burger" joint where the "finer white trash" hangs; sure, it can get a bit "loud and jostley", and the barkeep "might not use fresh lime juice" in your cosmo, but no one in the "eclectic" crowd gives a hoot.

Wall St. Kitchen & Bar   19 | 18 | 19 | $8
70 Broad St. (Beaver St.), 212-797-7070
■ After the closing bell, herds of "broker/trader" types head for this Financial District bar, one of the "only things open past 5 PM" in a nabe that sorely "lacks quality nightlife"; it's "so loud you can't hear yourself talk", but gals in the market for an "investment banker" shout it's pretty darn "great!"

Welcome to the Johnsons ⌿   19 | 20 | 17 | $5
123 Rivington St. (bet. Essex & Norfolk Sts.), 212-420-9911
◪ "Nostalgia ahoy" might be the motto of this "flashback" Lower Eastsider done up in a kitschy, "ultra-retro" style reminiscent of "someone's rec room in Ohio"; outsiders find it "not very welcoming" with "too many guys, as the name suggests", but brainiacs who think it's a "clever idea" make a mental note to "bring quarters for the Ms. Pac-Man."

Whiskey Ward   ▽ 22 | 17 | 22 | $5
121 Essex St. (bet. Delancey & Rivington Sts.), 212-477-2998
■ "Low-key" Lower Eastsider that takes its name from its location in the Fourth Ward (aka the 'Whiskey Ward' in days of yore); though unknown to many surveyors, this "great place to get the night started" offers the usual suspects – a "good jukebox, pool table and peanuts" – and a "quiet", serious-drinking ambiance.

Winnie's ⌿   ▽ 19 | 8 | 15 | $6
104 Bayard St. (bet. Baxter & Mulberry Sts.), 212-732-2384
■ "If you can find it", this "hole-in-the-wall" Chinatown "dive" is paradise for wanna-be warblers, who whinny along to some of the "best karaoke in the city" thanks to its mighty "good selection" of tunes; nevertheless, the "tacky videos" and "totally cheesy" decor strike a few discordant notes.

Nightlife A | D | S | C

Zinc Bar 22 | 19 | 18 | $7
90 W. Houston St. (bet. La Guardia Pl. & Thompson St.), 212-477-8337
■ "Red-hot" world jazz and ice-cold caipirinhas go down nicely together at this "intimate", "cave-like" SoHo lounge that has "cool and serene" written all over it; insiders settle into its "candlelit", Moorish-themed back room because it's "more relaxed" than the front bar, but no matter where you wind up, this "chill" choice is "worth the trek downstairs" and Downtown.

Zoë 21 | 20 | 20 | $9
90 Prince St. (bet. B'way & Mercer St.), 212-966-6722
■ Granted, most "go for the food", but a "quietly classy" ambiance also lures imbibers to this "upbeat" SoHo spot with a recently revamped bar; anticipate an "impressive" cocktail list designed by über-mixologist Dale DeGroff, a "pricey" but encyclopedic "selection of wines" and "good-looking folks aplenty", soaking it all in.

Nightlife Indexes

CATEGORIES
LOCATIONS
SPECIAL FEATURES

Indexes list the best of many within each category.

Nightlife Category Index

CATEGORIES

Bars
Anotheroom
Antarctica
Balthazar
Bar 89
Bayard's Blue Bar
Beckett's Bar & Grill
Blarney Stone
Blue Ribbon
bOb
Boom
Botanica Bar
Bridge Cafe
Broome St. Bar
Cafe Noir
Canteen
Chibi's Sake Bar
Circa Tabac
City Hall
Cub Room
Cupping Room Cafe
Dakota Roadhouse
Delmonico's Restaurant
Diva
Divine Bar
Donald Sacks
Dylan Prime
Ear Inn
Edward Moran
Eight Mile Creek
El Teddy's
Fanelli's Cafe
55 Wall
Flor de Sol
Full Shilling
Fun
Good World Bar & Grill
Grace
Harbour Lights
Harry's at Hanover Square
Idlewild
Iggy's Keltic Lounge
I Tre Merli
Jeremy's Ale House
John St. Bar & Grill
Kana
La Jumelle
Le Zinc
Liquor Store Bar
Living Room
Local 138
Lolita
L'Orange Bleue
Lotus Cafe
Lucky Strike
Ludlow Bar
M & R Bar
Mare Chiaro
Max Fish
Mehanata 416 B.C.
Meow Mix
Mercantile Grill
Merc Bar
Mercer Bar
Mexican Radio
Milady's
Milano's Bar
Milk and Honey
Mooza
Motor City Bar
Ñ
Naked Lunch
Nancy Whiskey
No Moore
Obeca Li
Odeon
Onieal's Grand Street
Orange Bear
Orchard Bar
Paris Cafe
Peasant
Pig N Whistle
Pravda
Puck Fair
Puffy's Tavern
Raccoon Lodge
Raoul's
Rivertown Lounge
Room
Sapphire Lounge
Screening Room
Southwest NY
Spring Lounge
Sugar
Sweet & Vicious
Swim
SX 137
Thom's Bar
Tja!
Toad Hall
Tribeca Grill
Tribeca Tavern

Nightlife Category Index

Vig Bar
Walker's
Wall St. Kitchen & Bar
Welcome to the Johnsons
Whiskey Ward
Zinc Bar
Zoë

Cabaret
RM
Shine
Slipper Room
Torch

Coffeehouses
Cafe Gitane
Cupping Room Cafe
Cyber Cafe
Kavehaz
Lotus Cafe
Pink Pony Cafe

Dance Clubs
Culture Club
Don Hill's
Mint
NV Bar/289 Lounge
Remy Lounge
RM
Sapphire Lounge
Shine
S.O.B.'s
205 Club
Vinyl

Karaoke
Arlene Grocery
Winnie's

Lounges
Angel
Barramundi
Bubble Lounge
Casa La Femme
Church Lounge
Denial
Double Happiness
Fun
Grand Bar
Kavehaz
Kush
Lansky Lounge
Laparue
Luna Lounge
Lush
Merc Bar
NV Bar/289 Lounge
Obeca Li
Onieal's Grand Street
Pravda
Recess
Red Bench
Remy Lounge
Rialto
Savoy
Slipper Room
Sugar
Sway
Swim
357
203 Spring St.
Velvet Restaurant
Veruka
Void

Music Clubs
Arlene Grocery
Bowery Ballroom
Knitting Factory
Living Room
Mercury Lounge
Tonic
Tribeca Blues

Sports Bar
Sporting Club

Strip Club
Baby Doll Lounge

Nightlife Location Index

LOCATIONS

Chinatown
Fun
Winnie's

Financial District
Bayard's Blue Bar
Beckett's B/G
Blarney Stone
Bridge Cafe
Dakota Roadhouse
Delmonico's
Divine Bar
Donald Sacks
Edward Moran
55 Wall
Full Shilling
Harbour Lights
Harry's Hanover Sq.
Jeremy's Ale
John St. B/G
Mercantile Grill
Orange Bear
Paris Cafe
Raccoon Lodge
SouthWest NY
Wall St. Kitchen

Little Italy
Botanica Bar
Cafe Gitane
Chibi's Sake Bar
Double Happiness
Eight Mile Creek
M & R Bar
Mare Chiaro
Mexican Radio
Milano's Bar
Onieal's
Peasant
Rialto
Spring Lounge
Sweet & Vicious
Velvet
Vig Bar

Lower East Side
Angel
Arlene Grocery
Barramundi
bOb
Bowery Ballroom
Good World B/G
Idlewild
Iggy's Keltic
Kush
Lansky Lounge
Living Room
Local 138
Lolita Bar
Lotus Cafe
Ludlow Bar
Luna Lounge
Max Fish
Meow Mix
Mercury Lounge
Milk and Honey
Mint
Mooza
Motor City Bar
Orchard Bar
Pink Pony
Rivertown Lounge
Sapphire Lounge
Slipper Room
Swim
SX 137
Tonic
Torch
205 Club
Welcome to the Johnsons
Whiskey Ward

SoHo
Antarctica
Balthazar
Bar 89
Blue Ribbon
Boom
Broome St. Bar
Cafe Noir
Canteen
Casa La Femme
Circa Tabac
Cub Room
Culture Club
Cupping Room Cafe
Cyber Cafe
Denial
Diva
Don Hill's
Ear Inn
Fanelli's Cafe
Grand Bar
I Tre Merli

Nightlife Location Index

Kaña
Kavehaz
La Jumelle
L'Orange Bleue
Lucky Strike
Merc Bar
Mercer Bar
Milady's
Ñ
Naked Lunch
NV Bar/289 Lounge
Pravda
Puck Fair
Raoul's
Recess
Red Bench
Room
Savoy
S.O.B.'s
Sway
Thom's Bar
357
Toad Hall
203 Spring St.
Veruka
Void
Zinc Bar
Zoë

TriBeCa
Anotheroom
Baby Doll Lounge
Bubble Lounge
Church Lounge
City Hall
Dylan Prime
El Teddy's
Flor de Sol
Grace
Independent, The
Knitting Factory
Laparue
Le Zinc
Liquor Store Bar
Lush
Mehanata 416 BC
Nancy Whiskey
No Moore
Obeca Li
Odeon
Pig N Whistle
Puffy's Tavern
Remy Lounge
RM
Screening Room
Shine
Sporting Club
Sugar
Tja!
Tribeca Blues
Tribeca Grill
Tribeca Tavern
Vinyl
Walker's

Nightlife Special Feature Index

SPECIAL FEATURES

After Work
Antarctica
Bayard's Blue Bar
Beckett's
Bubble Lounge
Canteen
Church Lounge
City Hall
Cub Room
Delmonico's
Divine Bar
Donald Sacks
Edward Moran
El Teddy's
55 Wall
Grace
Grand Bar
Harbour Lights
Harry's at Hanover Square
Jeremy's Ale House
John Street Bar
Liquor Store Bar
Mercantile Grill
Orange Bear
Pig N Whistle
SouthWest NY
Sugar
Tribeca Grill
Tribeca Tavern
Walker's
Wall St. Kitchen

Beautiful People
Balthazar
Blue Ribbon
Cafe Gitane
Cafe Noir
Canteen
Casa La Femme
Grand Bar
I Tre Merli
Laparue
Mint
Odeon
Peasant
Pravda
Raoul's
Rialto
Sway
Thom's Bar
Tja!

203 Spring St.
Velvet Restaurant
Veruka

Beer Specialists
Anotheroom
Bayard's Blue Bar
Good World B/G
Iggy's Keltic Lounge
Jeremy's Ale House
Paris Cafe
Puck Fair
Room, The
Sporting Club
Wall St. Kitchen

Champagne Specialists
Bubble Lounge
357

Cigar Friendly
Angel
Anotheroom
Antarctica
Baby Doll Lounge
Bar 89
Barramundi
Bayard's Blue Bar
Boom
Broome St. Bar
Cafe Noir
Casa La Femme
Church Lounge
Circa Tabac
Delmonico's
Divine Bar
Dylan Prime
Edward Moran
Eight Mile Creek
Fanelli's Cafe
55 Wall
Full Shilling
Harry's at Hanover Square
Independent, The
Jeremy's Ale House
John St. Bar
Kavehaz
L'Orange Bleue
Lush
Mare Chiaro
Mercantile Grill
Mint

Nightlife Special Feature Index

No Moore
NVBar/289 Lounge
Onieal's Grand Street
Paris Cafe
Pig N Whistle
Pravda
Puck Fair
Puffy's Tavern
Sapphire Lounge
Toad Hall
Torch
203 Spring St.
Velvet Restaurant
Veruka
Walker's
Wall St. Kitchen

Cocktail Experts
Cafe Noir
Church Lounge
City Hall
Double Happiness
Dylan Prime
Good World B/G
Independent, The
Kavehaz
Lansky Lounge
Le Zinc
Lucky Strike
M & R Bar
Milk and Honey
Pravda
Recess
Rialto
RM
Slipper Room
Tja!
Torch
Zoë

Cool Loos
Anotheroom
Bar 89
City Hall
Fun
Idlewild
SX 137

Dives
Antarctica
Baby Doll Lounge
Blarney Stone
Dakota Roadhouse
Don Hill's

Ear Inn
Jeremy's Ale House
Mare Chiaro
Milady's
Milano's Bar
Motor City Bar
Nancy Whiskey
Orange Bear
Paris Cafe
Puffy's Tavern
Raccoon Lodge

DJs
Angel
Anotheroom
bOb
Boom
Botanica Bar
Bubble Lounge
Culture Club
Denial
Don Hill's
Double Happiness
Dylan Prime
Fun
Good World B/G
Grand Bar
Idlewild
Independent, The
I Tre Merli
Kaña
Kush
Lansky Lounge
Laparue
Lotus Cafe
Lucky Strike
Ludlow Bar
Lush
M & R Bar
Mehanata 416 B.C.
Mint
Motor City Bar
Naked Lunch
NVBar/289 Lounge
Orchard Bar
Pravda
Puck Fair
Recess
Remy Lounge
Rivertown Lounge
RM
Sapphire Lounge
Shine
Slipper Room

Nightlife Special Feature Index

S.O.B.'s
Sugar
Sway
Swim
357
Tja!
205 Club
203 Spring St.
Velvet Restaurant
Veruka
Vig Bar
Vinyl
Void
Whiskey Ward

Eye Openers
(Serving at 8 AM)
Balthazar
Blarney Stone
Cupping Room Cafe
Jeremy's Ale House
Spring Lounge

Group Friendly
Antarctica
Bar 89
Casa La Femme
Church Lounge
Culture Club
Idlewild
Kaña
No Moore
Puck Fair
Sweet & Vicious
Winnie's

Grown-Ups
Bayard's Blue Bar
Delmonico's
Fanelli's Cafe
Harry's at Hanover Square
Le Zinc
Liquor Store Bar
Tribeca Grill

Happy Hour
Antarctica
Barramundi
bOb
Botanica Bar
Donald Sacks
Double Happiness
Ear Inn
Eight Mile Creek
55 Wall

Flor de Sol
Harbour Lights
Jeremy's Ale House
John Street Bar
Knitting Factory
Laparue
Local 138
Lolita
Ludlow Bar
Lush
M & R Bar
Meow Mix
Mooza
Motor City Bar
Naked Lunch
Nancy Whiskey
Onieal's Grand Street
Raccoon Lodge
Recess
Remy Lounge
Rivertown Lounge
RM
Sapphire Lounge
SouthWest NY
Sporting Club
Spring Lounge
Sweet & Vicious
Swim
205 Club
203 Spring St.
Welcome to the Johnsons
Whiskey Ward

Hotel Bars
Mercer Hotel
   Mercer Bar
Regent Wall St.
   55 Wall
60 Thompson Hotel
   Thom's Bar
SoHo Grand
   Grand Bar
Tribeca Grand
   Church Lounge

Irish
Beckett's
Blarney Stone
Full Shilling
Iggy's Keltic Lounge
Local 138
Pig N Whistle
Puck Fair

Nightlife Special Feature Index

Jukeboxes
Antarctica
Blarney Stone
Botanica Bar
Broome St. Bar
Dakota Roadhouse
Full Shilling
Jeremy's Ale House
Luna Lounge
Mare Chiaro
Max Fish
Mehanata 416 B.C.
Mercantile Grill
Mercury Lounge
Milano's Bar
Nancy Whiskey
Paris Cafe
Pig N Whistle
Pink Pony Cafe
Puffy's Tavern
Raccoon Lodge
Rivertown Lounge
Spring Lounge
Toad Hall
205 Club
Welcome to the Johnsons
Whiskey Ward

Meat Markets
Balthazar
Bar 89
bOb
Bubble Lounge
Cafe Noir
Canteen
Church Lounge
Cub Room
Culture Club
Divine Bar
Double Happiness
Edward Moran
El Teddy's
Grand Bar
Idlewild
I Tre Merli
Kush
La Jumelle
Lansky Lounge
Lucky Strike
Lush
Merc Bar
Mercer Bar
Naked Lunch
NVBar/289 Lounge
Pravda
Puck Fair
Rivertown Lounge
S.O.B.'s
Spring Lounge
Sugar
Sweet & Vicious

Noteworthy Newcomers
Laparue
Le Zinc
Lolita
Mint
Mooza
RM
Sugar
SX 137
Thom's Bar

Old New York
(50+ yrs; year opened;
* building)
1794 Bridge Cafe*
1817 Ear Inn
1842 55 Wall*
1851 Bayard's Blue Bar*
1851 Harry's at Hanover Square*
1863 City Hall*
1872 Fanelli's Cafe
1873 Paris Cafe
1890 Walker's*
1891 Delmonico's*
1908 Mare Chiaro
1923 Milady's
1945 Puffy's Tavern

Outdoor
Barramundi
Edward Moran
El Teddy's
55 Wall
Flor de Sol
Good World B/G
Harbour Lights
Independent, The
Kaña
M & R Bar
Mooza
Odeon
Raoul's
Rialto
SouthWest NY
Sweet & Vicious
Tribeca Grill

www.zagat.com

Nightlife Special Feature Index

Pub Grub
Beckett's
Blarney Stone
Bridge Cafe
Broome St. Bar
Dakota Roadhouse
Ear Inn
Edward Moran
Fanelli's Cafe
Jeremy's Ale House
John Street Bar
Mercantile Grill
Milady's
Nancy Whiskey
Paris Cafe
Pig N Whistle
Puck Fair
Puffy's Tavern
Walker's
Wall St. Kitchen

Romantic
Angel
Balthazar
Bubble Lounge
Cafe Noir
Casa La Femme
Circa Tabac
Double Happiness
Flor de Sol
I Tre Merli
Kush
Onieal's Grand Street
Raoul's
Room, The
Savoy
Torch
Velvet Restaurant
Zoë

Suits
Bayard's Blue Bar
Beckett's
Church Lounge
City Hall
Cub Room
Delmonico's
Divine Bar
Donald Sacks
Edward Moran
55 Wall
Full Shilling
Harry's at Hanover Square
Jeremy's Ale House
John St. Bar
Mercantile Grill
SouthWest NY
Tribeca Grill
Wall St. Kitchen

Swanky
Balthazar
Boom
Canteen
Church Lounge
Dylan Prime
Grace
Grand Bar
Lansky Lounge
Mercer Bar
Milk and Honey
Mint
NVBar/289 Lounge
Obeca Li
Raoul's
Thom's Bar
Torch
203 Spring St.

Tourist Favorites
Balthazar
Cub Room
Culture Club
Diva
Fanelli's Cafe
Grand Bar
Harbour Lights
Jeremy's Ale House
La Jumelle
Lucky Strike
Mare Chiaro
Mercer Bar

Trendy
Balthazar
Blue Ribbon
Cafe Gitane
Canteen
Church Lounge
Denial
Double Happiness
Fun
Good World B/G
Grace
Grand Bar
I Tre Merli
Laparue
Lush

Nightlife Special Feature Index

Mercer Bar
Mint
NVBar/289 Lounge
Odeon
Pravda
Red Bench
RM
Shine
Sugar
Sway
Swim
SX 137
357
Tja!
Tonic
205 Club
203 Spring St.
Veruka

Velvet Rope
Denial
Don Hill's
Fun
Idlewild
Kush
Lansky Lounge
Laparue
Lush
Mint

Naked Lunch
NVBar/289 Lounge
Pravda
RM
Shine
Sway
357
205 Club
203 Spring St.
Veruka
Vinyl

Wine Bars
Anotheroom
Divine Bar
Room, The
Von

Wine by the Glass
Anotheroom
Divine Bar
Harry's at Hanover Square
Kavehaz
Ñ
Room, The
Tribeca Grill
Wall St. Kitchen
Zoë

Shopping

Shopping Map

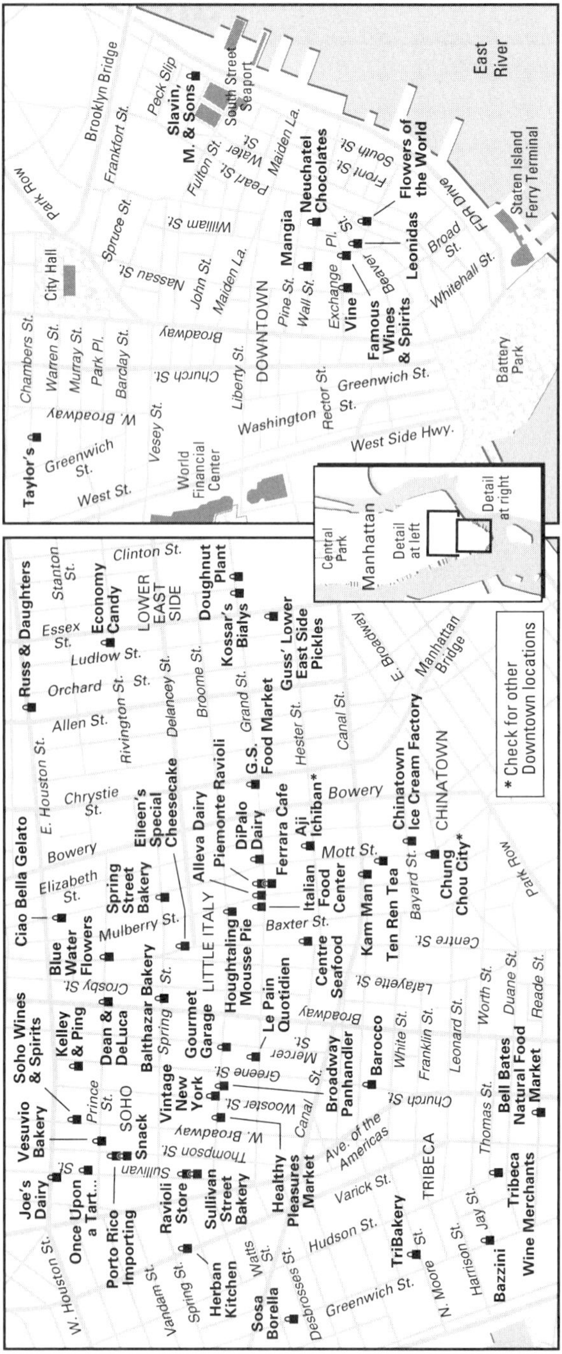

Top Rated Shops

Listed in order of Overall rating

Breads
- 24 Sullivan St. Bakery
- 23 Balthazar Bakery
    Dean & DeLuca
    Le Pain Quotidien

Cakes/Pies
- 27 Sylvia Weinstock Cakes
- 24 Baked Ideas*
- 23 Bijoux Doux*
    Houghtaling Mousse Pie*

Candy & Nuts
- 26 Leonidas
- 25 Kadouri & Sons*
    Neuchatel Chocolates
- 24 Economy Candy

Caterers & Event Planners
- 24 Great Performances
    Charlotte's Catering*
    Food in Motion*
- 23 Dean & DeLuca

Cheese & Dairy
- 26 DiPalo Dairy
- 25 Dean & DeLuca
- 24 Joe's Dairy
    Alleva Dairy

Coffee & Tea
- 25 Porto Rico Importing
    Ten Ren Tea
- 23 Dean & DeLuca
- 22 Bell Bates Natural Market

Cookies
- 24 Baked Ideas*
- 23 Duane Park Patisserie
- 22 Taylor's
- 19 Ferrara

Cookware & Supplies
- 24 Broadway Panhandler
- 21 Dean & DeLuca
    Bari Restaurant Equipment
    Matas Restaurant Supply*

Fish
- 23 Slavin, M. & Sons
    Dean & DeLuca
- 21 G.S. Food Market
- 20 Hai Thanh Seafood*

Food Specialty Shops
- 24 Dean & DeLuca
- 21 Gourmet Garage
    Italian Food Center
- 20 Kam Man

Ice Cream
- 24 Ciao Bella Gelato
- 22 Häagen Dazs
    Chinatown Ice Cream
- 19 Baskin-Robbins

Meat & Poultry
- 24 Dean & DeLuca
- 22 Catherine St. Meat Market*
- 21 Bayard St. Meat Market*
- 20 Grand St. Sausages*

Overall
- 27 Sylvia Weinstock Cakes
- 26 DiPalo Dairy
    Leonidas
    Russ & Daughters

Pastas
- 26 DiPalo Dairy
- 24 Piemonte Ravioli
    Ravioli Store
- 23 Dean & DeLuca

Pastries
- 23 Balthazar Bakery
    Ceci-Cela
    Dean & DeLuca
    Duane Park Patisserie

Prepared Foods
- 24 Sosa Borella*
- 23 Dean & DeLuca
    Mangia
- 22 Daily Soup

---

* Low votes

www.zagat.com   103

Key to Ratings/Symbols

Name, Address & Phone Number

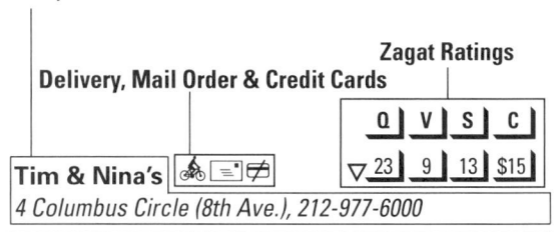

Delivery, Mail Order & Credit Cards

Zagat Ratings

Q	V	S	C
▽ 23	9	13	$15

Tim & Nina's
4 Columbus Circle (8th Ave.), 212-977-6000

◪ It's either feast or famine at this "wildly inconsistent" Columbus Circle prepared foods specialist; hit it at the right time and you'll find anything from "finger-lickin'" BBQ to "premier" pastas to "super" sushi, but on a bad day your options may be limited to "stale" cookies and "melted" ice cream; 24-hour service is "convenient", but may also help explain the "sleepwalking" staff.

Review, with surveyors' comments in quotes

Before each review a symbol indicates whether responses were uniform ■ or mixed ◪.

Establishments with the highest overall ratings and greatest popularity and importance are printed in CAPITAL LETTERS.

Delivery: 🚲 delivery available
Mail Order: ✉ mail order available
Credit Cards: ⊘ no credit cards accepted

Ratings: Quality, Variety and Service are rated on a scale of **0** to **30.** The Cost (C) column reflects our surveyors' estimate of the price range.

Q	Quality	V	Variety	S	Service	C	Cost
23		9		13		$15	

0–9 poor to fair
10–15 fair to good
16–19 good to very good
20–25 very good to excellent
26–30 extraordinary to perfection
▽ low response/less reliable

For places listed without ratings or a cost estimate, such as an important **newcomer** or a popular **write-in,** the estimated cost is indicated by the following symbols.

I   Inexpensive
M   Moderate
E   Expensive
VE Very Expensive

www.zagat.com

Shopping Q | V | S | C

Aji Ichiban – | – | – | I
37 Mott St. (bet. Bayard & Doyers Sts.), 212-233-7650
167 Hester St. (bet. Elizabeth & Mott Sts.), 212-925-1133
www.Ajiichiban-usa.com
Expand your definition of candies and snacks with a visit to these fascinating Downtown sweet and savory shops, franchises of a Hong Kong–based company; while their offerings are from around the world, they specialize in Asian items, specifically dried seafood and fruit like roasted fish crisps and salted kumquats; N.B. since some items are an acquired taste, samples of everything are offered.

Alleva Dairy ✉ 27 | 21 | 23 | M
188 Grand St. (Mulberry St.), 212-226-7990, 800-425-5382
■ One of the oldest Italian cheese stores in the country (born in 1892), this "consistently good" "Little Italy stalwart" is "an old-fashioned dairy" that keeps its customers crooning with "homemade" mozzarella and ricotta that are "as smooth as a Verdi aria."

Baked Ideas 🚲 ✉ ▽ 23 | 24 | 24 | E
450 Broadway (Grand St.), 212-925-9097
■ "You design it", they'll make it say patrons of this baker who creates cakes and cookies in any shape imaginable, from a company logo to wow the boss to an image of your beloved – the icing on the cake for a romantic evening.

BALTHAZAR BAKERY 🚲 ✉ 27 | 22 | 21 | E
80 Spring St. (bet. B'way & Crosby St.), 212-965-1785
www.balthazarny.com
■ At this "very classy", "true Parisian" bakery next door to the sceney SoHo restaurant, look for "crusty, light" baguettes, "*magnifique*" Valrhona chocolate bread, "excellent" fruit focaccia, brioche and tarts; despite complaints of "snooty" service, "cramped" quarters and high prices, most judge it "superb, in spite of the hype."

Bari Restaurant Equipment 🚲 ✉ 23 | 23 | 18 | M
240 Bowery (bet. Houston & Prince Sts.), 212-925-3845
www.bariequipment.com
■ This Bowery institution supplies restaurants and home chefs with all the necessities – "if they don't carry it, it doesn't exist"; it's "the pro's choice" for "good quality at reasonable prices", and if some find it "disorganized", the bottom line is "if you need a whisk the length of your leg, it's there."

Barocco 🚲 22 | 18 | 19 | M
297 Church St. (bet. Walker & White Sts.), 212-431-0065
■ Despite a "limited selection", this TriBeCa venue makes a good impression with its "reliable", "good quality" prepared food offerings; regulars say "try the lasagna" (vegetable or meat), salad combo and sandwiches, and be sure to leave room for the "richest bread pudding around."

Shopping   Q | V | S | C

Barraud Caterers ⌐   _ | _ | _ | E
*405 Broome St. (bet. Centre & Lafayette Sts.),
212-925-1334*
Rosemary Howe, chef-owner of this firm specializing in smaller events (dinners for up to 200, cocktails up to 800), designs Eclectic menus that reflect her creative talents (she's a former drama teacher) as well as her varied culinary background: born in India, she trained in Europe and worked as a private chef before establishing her business in 1980; everything she serves is handmade, and she also offers wine consultations and etiquette advice.

Baskin-Robbins ⌐   19 | 22 | 17 | I
*355 Grand St. (Essex St.), 212-777-8785
www.baskinrobbins.com*
◪ Famous for its "31-derful flavors", this "old-time favorite" may get the cold shoulder from scoop snobs who will eat the "insultingly small" dips of "Middle America's ice cream" only "if desperate", but loyalists swear by the "out-of-this-world" mint chocolate chip as well as "cute" specialty cakes that "bring back childhood memories."

Bayard Street Meat Market 🚴⌐ ▽   23 | 22 | 17 | I
57 Bayard St. (Elizabeth St.), 212-619-6206
■ It's "worth a trip Downtown" to check out the "astounding selection" of fresh meats and fowl at this "fast and friendly" Chinatown market, which serves locals as well as folks from around town in search of "best deals"; besides the standards it offers "exotic cuts hard to find elsewhere."

Bazzini, A.L., Co. 🚴✉   26 | 24 | 20 | M
339 Greenwich St. (Jay St.), 212-334-1280
■ "You may see De Niro" stocking up at this more than 100-year-old TriBeCa store with a variety of "delectable" nuts and dried fruits at "fair prices"; fans say "nothing beats their chocolate-coated almonds" and "best cashews."

Bell Bates
Natural Food Market 🚴✉   23 | 25 | 18 | M
*97 Reade St. (bet. Church St. & W. B'way), 212-267-4300
www.bellbates.com*
■ This "large and airy" TriBeCa standby offers "jillions of items", including the "best selection" of herbs, spices, coffees and herbal teas, plus organic produce, a deli and a juice bar; it might be a "secret to most NYers", but it's a "real find" for "good value."

Bijoux Doux
Specialty Cakes 🚴✉⌐   ▽ 26 | 23 | 21 | E
*304 Mulberry St. (bet. Bleecker & Houston Sts.),
212-226-0948*
■ Custom-made cakes in a variety of price ranges are the hallmarks of this baker with a luscious repertoire of layers, fillings and icings; the results really are like edible *bijoux*.

Shopping   Q | V | S | C

Blue Water Flowers   – | – | – | E
265 Lafayette St. (bet. Prince & Spring Sts.), 212-226-0587
www.bluewaterflowers.com
A bench out front for weary locals, a creaky door and a homey, hand-painted interior with dogs scurrying about fuel the neighborhood warmth of this charming SoHo florist whose owner has a knack for unusually hued arrangements set in glass ginger jars; not content with carnations, gladioli or red roses, the bouquets often star hydrangeas from Holland, colored calla lillies and peonies; topiary and dried flower ornaments in unusual shapes (hearts, candy canes) are other specialties.

Bridgewaters   21 | 21 | 21 | E
11 Fulton St. (bet. South & Water Sts.), 212-608-8823
www.bridgewatersnyc.com
◪ "Go for the view" sums up the chief attraction of this "spacious" American catering facility at the South Street Seaport, offering a harborside and Brooklyn Bridge view from the wraparound terrace (available in summer for outdoor BBQs); other pluses include "standard" but "good" food and a "competent" staff – just watch out for the "expensive" tab.

BROADWAY PANHANDLER ✉   27 | 25 | 21 | M
477 Broome St. (bet. Greene & Wooster Sts.), 212-966-3434
■ SoHo's "fairyland" for kitchen mavens offers "good discounts" on "serious cookware" and is especially "great for baking supplies"; it also has its share of "expensive kitchen toys" and "funky home gadgets", making it an "interesting" gift source, and service is generally "helpful."

Caffé Roma Pastry ⊄   21 | 20 | 18 | M
385 Broome St. (Mulberry St.), 212-226-8413
◪ "Old-world sensibilities" pervade this "step back in time", a "quintessential Little Italy" coffeehouse/bakery offering "classic Italian pastries", homemade gelati and the like; it's also a nice "spot to relax" with a cappuccino, but a few less enthralled patrons say "great setting, mundane fare."

Catherine Street Meat Market ⊄ ▽ 22 | 22 | 21 | I
21 Catherine St. (E. B'way), 212-693-0494
◪ This Chinatown shop's "wide selection" includes "tripe and other internals" ("stay away if you're squeamish") as well as more conventional meats; fans cite "good quality", others say "nothing special", but there's no question prices are reasonable.

Ceci-Cela   26 | 22 | 22 | M
55 Spring St. (bet. Lafayette & Mulberry Sts.), 212-274-9179
■ "Thoroughbred" lemon tarts and "seminal" almond croissants are highlights among the "cruelly delicious" goods at this "neighborhood" French patisserie in Little Italy that's "truly authentic" yet has "no attitude."

www.zagat.com

Shopping   Q | V | S | C

Centre Seafood 🚴 🚫   - | - | - | M
(fka A.E.G. Seafood)
206 Centre St. (bet. Grand & Hester Sts.), 212-966-6299
Occupying a long warehouse space lined with huge saltwater tanks, this Chinatown wholesaler is known for "fair prices" on lobsters of all sizes, plus live cod, striped bass and Dungeness crab; old hands stop here for the "worthwhile" retail specials on live fish and shellfish, as they don't sell fillets – nor do they scale and clean.

Charlotte's Catering   ∇ 24 | 24 | 24 | E
146 Chambers St. (bet. Greenwich St. & W. B'way), 212-732-7939
■ From scouting the ideal locale to providing flowers, music and lighting, this "well-organized" full-service event planner takes care of all the details; whether for a cozy tea or a large dinner-dance, "the food is spectacular, creative" and "beautifully presented"; combined with "professional, friendly" service, "it's well worth the price."

Chinatown Ice Cream Factory 🚫   23 | 23 | 19 | I
65 Bayard St. (bet. Elizabeth & Mott Sts.), 212-608-4170
■ This "Chinatown must" makes its own ice cream in "exotic flavors you can't get elsewhere" (e.g. taro, ginger, litchi, red bean and green tea – "if it freezes, it's here"); finicky types appreciate that "you can ask for samples first" at this "one of a kind" dessert "adventure."

Chung Chou City   - | - | - | VE
39 Mott St. (Pell St.), 212-285-2288
218-220 Grand St. (Elizabeth St.), 212-274-9338
These C-town markets offer dried items, many displayed like jewels in glass jars; don't load up on the birds' nests, since at a starting price of $130 an ounce you won't have money left for the likes of dried sea dragons, abalone or shark fins.

CIAO BELLA GELATO 🚫   27 | 23 | 21 | M
285 Mott St. (bet. E. Houston & Prince Sts.), 212-431-3591
www.ciaobellagelato.com
■ The "unbelievably addictive", "very decadent" sorbetto and gelato at this NoLita shop are "worth sinning for", and transgressors shout "*molto bene!*"; while penitents murmur "the prices make your stomach sink", most agree the "fresh, fruity flavors" are "perfection in a cup."

Columbine 🚴   - | - | - | M
229 W. Broadway (White St.), 212-965-0909
TriBeCa locals line up at this tiny shop that produces flavorful soups, salads and sandwiches; offerings include the likes of a sweet and savory jerk chicken sandwich, new potato salad and 'mad Martha's' chocolate-cherry cookie.

Connecticut Muffin 🚫   18 | 20 | 18 | I
10 Prince St. (bet. Bowery & Elizabeth St.), 212-925-9773
◪ To supporters, this Little Italy bakery offers a "good choice" of "nice", if "generic", "chain-style" muffins,

Shopping Q | V | S | C

cookies and scones; however, critics cite "inconsistent taste" and say it "belongs in a mall, not NYC."

Daily Soup 🚲 🚭   24 | 23 | 20 | M
55 Broad St. (Beaver St.), 212-222-7687
www.dailysoup.com
▰ A "great variety" of "inventive" soups (including low-fat, vegetarian and nondairy options) draws lunchtime lines to this Downtown soup spot staffed by "nice people"; penny-pinchers gravitate toward the 'blue pot special' or go after 3 PM, when 12-ounce cups are $3; N.B. this is the only remaining independently owned Daily Soup.

DEAN & DELUCA 🚲 🖃   27 | 26 | 21 | E
560 Broadway (Prince St.), 212-431-1691, 800-221-7714
www.deandeluca.com
■ "The Lamborghini of markets – fun to look at and dream about, impossible to afford" sums up this SoHo shop; it's "excellent" in "most departments" (especially produce and cheese) and has things "you won't find" elsewhere, so even if you "leave much poorer", it's "worth it."

Deb's 🚲   – | – | – | M
200 Varick St. (bet. Houston & King Sts.), 212-675-4550
If not for the midday bustle at this bright little take-out/catering joint in SoHo, one might linger longer in delicious indecision over the mouthwatering array of changing Eclectic options – in addition to seasonal soups and creative salads, sandwiches and wraps, there are hot entrees plus fresh-baked goodies for a sweet finale.

DIPALO DAIRY   29 | 24 | 25 | I
206 Grand St. (Mott St.), 212-226-1033
■ There's "always a line" at "Little Italy's best" cheese shop (rated No. 1 for Quality), but few seem to mind, since "you're treated like family" by folks "who are passionate about their product" and will give you "some Parmigiano-Reggiano to nibble on" while you wait; whether it's the "excellent ricotta" or mozzarella, "everything tastes better here" – or maybe, as one besotted fan whispers, "it's love!"

Donald Sacks 🚲   20 | 18 | 17 | E
World Financial Ctr., 220 Vesey St. (West St.), 212-619-4600
▰ This WFC eatery/take-out shop fuels financial types with "decent sandwiches" and other "good quality" fare, though after crunching the numbers some conservative spenders rate it pricey; **N.B. closed at press time.**

Doughnut Plant 🚲 🚭   – | – | – | I
379 Grand St. (bet. Essex & Norfolk Sts.), 212-505-3700
www.doughnutplant.com
Mark Isreal may not wake up each day and think 'time to make the doughnuts', but one peek inside his Lower East Side shop and you'll know it's time to eat the doughnuts; his glazed treats (in the original Tahitian vanilla bean flavor

www.zagat.com   109

Shopping

and a rotation of others such as Key lime or Valrhona chocolate) are made from scratch, following an old family recipe, and though the plant closes as soon as they're sold out, you can also find his doughnuts at some gourmet shops.

Duane Park Patisserie | 26 | 21 | 22 | E |
179 Duane St. (bet. Greenwich & Hudson Sts.), 212-274-8447
www.madelines.net
■ Whether strolling in to "check out their cookies" or picking up some "upscale" American, Viennese or French pastries, you'll agree that this TriBeCa "gem" offers a "limited" but "elegant and artful" selection of goods – for which you'll pay; all in all, it's "another find for the area"; N.B. closed Sundays in summer.

Economy Candy | 25 | 27 | 21 | I |
108 Rivington St. (bet. Essex & Ludlow Sts.), 212-254-1531, 800-352-4544
www.economycandy.com
■ "Dentists owe a debt of gratitude" to this Lower East Side "landmark" ("no other place like it") that's "a great source for bulk candy", dried fruits, nuts and "halvah cut to order", all at "low prices"; "you could lose your mind there's so much stuff" and the interior's definitely "not elegant", but that's the charm for many who call it "just plain fun" – "I feel like a kid in a penny candy store."

Eileen's Special Cheesecake | 25 | 21 | 21 | M |
17 Cleveland Pl. (Centre & Kenmare Sts.), 212-966-5585
www.eileencheesecake.com
■ "Creamy, dreamy" cheesecakes in a "smorgasbord" of flavors are the draw at this Little Italy one-note bakery; while sticklers judge it "almost as good as Junior's", devotees insist "there is no better"; Balducci's also stocks their line, and they offer overnight delivery anywhere in the U.S.

Famous Wines & Spirits | ▽ | 25 | 23 | 23 | M |
40 Exchange Pl. (William St.), 212-422-4743
www.famouswines.com
■ Wall Streeters have shopped at this "friendly" store for over 60 years; with its "good suggestions" and "reasonable prices", it's "the place to go when you want a good bottle but don't want to mortgage the house."

Ferrara | 20 | 22 | 17 | M |
195 Grand St. (bet. Mott & Mulberry Sts.), 212-226-6150
www.ferraracafe.com
◪ Although one of NY's oldest pasticcerias (circa 1892) has expanded beyond its Little Italy home, it's still this Grand Street original that's the "standout", a "sentimental favorite" where fans head for the "king of cannoli" and other "delicious desserts"; critics may grouse that it has "seen better days", but it's still "excellent after Peking duck – da neighborhood's changed, ok?"

Shopping   Q | V | S | C

Flowers of the World 🚴   24 | 23 | 21 | M
(fka Broadway Floral Exchange)
5 Hanover Sq. (bet. Pearl & William Sts.), 212-425-2234, 800-770-3119
■ A "decent" bet Downtown, this Wall Streeter offers "lovely bouquets" of "fresh, beautiful" blooms plus fruit and gourmet baskets; it's handy when in need of a "quick" gift or floral fix at a "reasonable" price.

Fong Inn Too 🚴⌀   – | – | – | M
46 Mott St. (bet. Bayard & Pell Sts.), 212-962-5196
Take a quick trip to China via this elemental Chinatown food specialty shop; bring cash, be ready to fight your way to the front and deal with a language barrier and you can walk out with the basics (noodles, bean curd, rice cakes) at basic prices.

Food in Motion ⌀   ∇ 24 | 24 | 23 | E
148 Chambers St. (bet. Greenwich St. & W. B'way), 212-766-4400
■ "Great for huge events", this Eclectic caterer/event planner is in its element designing corporate galas for hundreds (i.e. a sit-down dinner for 800 in Grand Central Station), but it's also "superb" for smaller affairs such as a buffet lunch for 25 or a private dinner party for 10.

Gertel's Bake Shop 🚴 ✉   21 | 20 | 18 | M
53 Hester St. (bet. Essex & Ludlow Sts.), 212-982-3250
◪ In business since 1918, this "Lower East Side landmark" is "the place to shop" "when it has to be kosher" insist fans; though a few foes swear the goods "tasted better when I was a kid", most "love the babka" and claim they achieve "miracles at Passover."

Godiva Chocolatier 🚴 ✉   25 | 24 | 23 | E
World Financial Ctr., 225 Liberty St., Winter Garden, 212-945-2174
33 Maiden Ln. (Nassau St.), 212-809-8990
South St. Seaport, 21 Fulton St. (bet. Pearl & Water Sts.), 212-571-6965
www.godiva.com
◪ More than 3,000 surveyors voted on this chain that's "a little '80s" but offers "dependable" "high-quality" chocolates that are a "wonderful indulgence"; the less enthused say "boring", "commercial" and "not worth the money", but for legions, the "name and packaging still do the trick"; **N.B. the WFC branch is closed at press time.**

Gourmet Garage 🚴   23 | 22 | 18 | M
453 Broome St. (Mercer St.), 212-941-5850
www.gourmetgarage.com
◪ "Not everything is a bargain" and both quality and variety can be "somewhat erratic", but this no-frills gourmet market offers "good basics", fresh fish and meat, plus "some real finds", with praise for the produce, breads, store-brand items and "delicious selection of olives."

www.zagat.com

Shopping   Q | V | S | C

Grand Street Sausages ⊉   ▽ 23 | 20 | 18 | I
198 Grand St. (bet. Mott & Mulberry Sts.), 212-966-3033
■ Connoisseurs call this Little Italy meat market a great source for "mysterious body parts" (cured pork tongue, duck feet), but if your needs are more mundane, you'll also find "delicious" sausages, beef and more at "good prices"; that "locals" shop here is taken as a good sign.

Great Performances   24 | 24 | 25 | E
287 Spring St. (Hudson St.), 212-727-2424
www.greatperformances.com
■ Focusing on the corporate market, this "professional", "eager-to-please" caterer turns out "delicious" Regional American fare and can orchestrate every detail for events ranging from dinner for a dozen to a company picnic for 10,000; "reliable" and "great in all departments", it earns a double thumbs-up; N.B. the team also includes Ronnie Davis, who closed his highly regarded Washington Street Caterers a few years ago and joined Great Performances, bringing key staffers and clients along.

G.S. Food Market ⊉   ▽ 23 | 23 | 17 | M
(fka Ocean Star Market)
250 Grand St. (Chrystie St.), 212-274-0990
■ If the more than 10 varieties of shrimp don't do the trick, it's still "worth the trip" to this bustling Chinese market for its impressive array of snapper, halibut, sole, snails, clams, oysters, scallops and salmon, plus an extensive selection of frozen seafood; the "good service" is valuable for sorting it all out.

GUSS' LOWER   28 | 23 | 21 | I
EAST SIDE PICKLES ▣
35 Essex St. (Grand St.), 212-254-4477, 800-252-4877
www.gusspickles.com
■ "Never have cucumbers been put to better use" than at this "nostalgic" Lower East Side stand that elevates pickles to a "culinary art form" with a "well-priced" choice of "crisp, garlicky", "right-out-of-a-barrel" specimens; "heavenly" sauerkraut and horseradish that will "clear your sinuses" are more reasons why this "legend" still generates "long lines" and is "a must on any food lover's tour of NY."

Häagen Dazs 🚲   26 | 23 | 19 | M
South Street Seaport, 89 South St., Pier 17, 212-587-5335
53½ Mott St. (Bayard St.), 212-571-1970
www.haagendazs.com
■ "Proof positive that quality can be mass-produced", this national "crème de la crème" chain scoops out "the Mercedes of ice cream" plus "pretty darn good" frozen yogurt and "divine" sorbet ("try the chocolate"); "always rich, always decadent" and "almost worth the angioplasty", the "king of the cream" only takes a licking for "overpriced, stingy portions" and "not the most motivated staff."

Shopping   Q | V | S | C

Hai Thanh Seafood Co., Inc. 🚲 🚫 ▽ | 21 | 23 | 16 | I
17-B Catherine St. (E. B'way), 212-964-9694

◪ "More Americanized" than its neighborhood rivals, this Chinatown fish market delivers the same "terrific values" on live lobster, crab, carp and bass plus iced-down seafood on the sidewalk in front; although not many surveyors know it, a few opine that "selection and quality are not spectacular (though low prices are)", so "choose carefully."

HEALTHY PLEASURES MARKET 🚲 ▭ | 24 | 25 | 18 | M
489 Broome St. (W. B'way), 212-431-7434
www.healthypleasures.com

◪ "All a health store should be", this SoHo "godsend" offers a "terrific array" of products: "amazing organic produce", a "surprisingly good fish and meat counter" and a "great salad bar" – "if you can't find it here, you're in trouble", though some sniff the "help is not very helpful."

Herban Kitchen 🚲 | 23 | 20 | 21 | M
290 Hudson St. (bet. Dominick & Spring Sts.), 212-627-2257, 888-437-2261
www.herbankitchen.com

◼ Patrons praise this West SoHo eat-in/take-out place as an "oasis of health and herbs" with its "nicely prepared, low-fat selections" and other "great organic stuff"; a "laid-back" atmosphere prevails – wear your Birkenstocks.

Hong Kong Supermarket | 22 | 25 | 13 | I
109 E. Broadway (Pike St.), 212-227-3388

◼ This "huge" Chinese market offers a "cornucopia" of "cheap" "Asian goodies"; it's "fun to explore", but "go with a translator" or "don't count on help."

Houghtaling Mousse Pie Ltd. ▭ 🚫 | ▽ 27 | 19 | 22 | M
389 Broome St. (bet. Centre & Mulberry Sts.), 212-226-3724

◼ Renowned for their "extraterrestrial" chocolate mousse pies (which they supply to Peter Luger, among others), this Little Italy bakery may have "no bargains" but "everything is a treat", including their chocolate truffle products, so it's "worth the trip" (check out the mousse shakes).

Hung Chong Import 🚫 | ▽ 21 | 22 | 14 | I
14 Bowery (bet. Doyers & Pell Sts.), 646-831-3943

◼ Tidy but no-frills Chinatown shop carrying a "good selection" of cookware and kitchen gadgets – woks, pots, strainers, whisks, knives, baking pans, cleavers stamped with the company's own logo, etc.; service doesn't win high marks, but low prices compensate.

Italian Food Center 🚲 ▭ | 23 | 20 | 19 | M
186 Grand St. (Mulberry St.), 212-925-2954

◼ Little Italy's "best sandwiches bar none" ("the 'New Yorker' is *bellissimo*") are made at this Italian specialty

www.zagat.com   113

Shopping | Q | V | S | C |

foods shop that feels like a "country grocer in Sicily"; besides being "the real thing for hero sandwiches", it also sells "wonderful" sausages, "great deli meats", "fresh mozzarella", pastas and other "authentic" goods.

JOE'S DAIRY ⌿ | 28 | 19 | 24 | I |
156 Sullivan St. (bet. Houston & Prince Sts.), 212-677-8780
■ The scent of "tasty" homemade mozzarella "perfumes the whole block" around this "old-style Italian place in SoHo", attracting cheese lovers in search of "the best smoked mozzarella in town, period" at "fair prices"; partisans say "it doesn't get any better than this."

Kadouri & Sons | ▽ 26 | 26 | 24 | I |
51 Hester St. (bet. Essex & Ludlow Sts.), 212-677-5441
■ Devotees swear "heaven smells like" this "great bargain emporium on the Lower East Side" where the nuts, dried fruit and candy from the Middle East (along with exotic grains and spices) make "you feel like you're in a market in Jerusalem"; a "helpful staff" and an owner your bubbe insists is "a doll" are more reasons to head here.

Kam Kuo Food Corp. | 22 | 25 | 12 | I |
7 Mott St. (Park Row), 212-349-3098
■ "Nearly a carbon copy" of Kam Man but "without the crowds", this "economical" Chinatowner carries everything needed "for the serious Chinese cook", from produce, meat and staples to "bizarre treats"; there are Thai and Japanese items too, and "check out the utensils on the second floor."

Kam Man | 22 | 26 | 12 | I |
200 Canal St. (bet. Mott & Mulberry Sts.), 212-571-0330
■ "Whatever the recipe calls for, you'll find it" at this "quintessential Chinese supermarket", a big, bi-level Chinatown scene "packed with Asian spices, sauces", dried meat and fish plus other exotica; though the language barrier can pose problems, for "something different, this is the place."

Kelley & Ping | 22 | 21 | 19 | M |
127 Greene St. (bet. Houston & Prince Sts.), 212-228-1212
■ Tea mavens tout the "impressive" choice and savvy help at this "hip" Asian grocery/restaurant/take-out shop in SoHo, where the 15 "exotic" varieties, from Japanese Sencha to China Terry Souchong, can be sampled at the tea counter; though prices make some go "to Chinatown", you've a better "chance of bumping into a model" here.

KOSSAR'S BIALYS | 28 | 21 | 20 | I |
367 Grand St. (Essex St.), 212-473-4810
www.kossarsbialys.com
■ "Nobody does it better" croon devotees of this more than 60-year-old Lower East Side baker that produces the city's "definitive" bialy with "fresh onion ground by hand";

Shopping   Q | V | S | C

in addition to the "fabulous, floury" favorite, there are discs, bulkas and bagels at this "final link to old NYC" that deserves "landmark status."

LEONIDAS 🚴 ▭   27 | 26 | 24 | E
3 Hanover Sq. (Pearl St.), 212-422-9600
www.leonidas-chocolate.com
■ "Exquisite" pralines and the "best chocolate-covered orange peels" for less than at some other high-enders make this Belgian boutique a must for chocoholics in search of "wonderful quality for the money"; the "helpful staff" earns almost as much praise as the "tasty" candy, making this purveyor a "gem among chocolate shops."

Le Pain Quotidien ⊭   26 | 19 | 22 | E
100 Grand St. (Mercer St.), 212-625-9009
www.painquotidien.com
■ This SoHo outpost of the rapidly expanding French-Belgian bakery/cafe chain has quickly endeared itself to the neighborhood with its "sensational baguettes", "rustic, hearty breads", sandwiches, pastries and coffee, all served up in stylish digs – at very urban prices.

Little Place, The 🚴 🏍 ⊭   – | – | – | I
73 W. Broadway (bet. Murray & Warren Sts.), 212-528-3175
The name isn't the only thing they've got right at this tiny pink TriBeCa storefront – the cooks get the Mexican food right too, turning out vegetable wraps, cornbread, chicken tamales and other affordable take-out eats (seating is limited to a few swivel stools); the menu is as little as the place, but service comes with a great big smile.

Lung Moon Bakery ⊭   19 | 19 | 15 | I
83 Mulberry St. (bet. Canal & Bayard Sts.), 212-349-4945
◪ Tagged the "definitive choice for Chinese pastries" and "fresh-made mooncakes", this "old-time" Chinatown shop also wins points for its "reasonable prices"; while not everyone is bowled over ("ok for its type"), it offers items for both "the adventurous and the faint of heart", so those unfamiliar with black bean–paste cake may want to try it.

Mangia 🚴   25 | 24 | 20 | M
Trump Bldg., 40 Wall St. (bet. Broad & William Sts.), 212-425-4040
■ This sleek Mediterranean take-out/eat-in spot is an "addiction" for many thanks to its "unique" sandwiches, "fabulous soups", bargain pizzas and "amazing" salad bars; it's also "great" for office catering, which is one way to avoid the "overwhelming" lunch crowds.

Manna ⊭   ▽ 25 | 21 | 22 | E
24 Harrison St. (bet. Greenwich & Hudson Sts.), 212-966-3449
www.mannacatering.com
■ Though he's a high-profile kosher caterer, chef Dan Lenchner's cooking is inspired by an international array of cuisines and often takes a "healthy" approach; his "good

Shopping | Q | V | S | C |

service" has helped land such plum assignments as Steven Spielberg's wedding, as well as a wide array of cocktail receptions and benefit lunches and dinners.

Maria's Bakery ⌿ | 18 | 19 | 15 | I |
148 Lafayette St. (bet. Grand & Howard Sts.), 212-925-3833
42 Mott St. (bet. Bayard & Pell Sts.), 212-732-3888
◪ "Flaky and smooth egg custards", "good sponge cake" and a big variety of sweet and savory buns that are "light on your taste buds and wallet" are highlights at these Chinese bakeries that are "great places to experiment" despite a "mild communication problem"; but critics find the pastries too "Americanized" and others warn "it's an acquired taste."

Matas Restaurant Supply 🚲   ▽ | 23 | 24 | 18 | M |
210 Bowery (bet. Prince & Spring Sts.), 212-431-0625
◼ "Almost everything" is available at this Bowery supplier of retail and wholesale kitchenware and tabletop items; the "astounding" selection includes glassware, china, silverware, pots, pans and more, and if what you want isn't in stock, they can probably order it for you.

Moishe's Kosher Bake Shop ⌿ | 21 | 19 | 17 | I |
504 Grand St. (bet. Columbia & Willett Sts.), 212-673-5832
◼ "The best quality challah in Manhattan" and "outstanding hamantaschen" can be had at this Lower East Side "trip back in time" to the "classic Jewish breads and pastries" of yesteryear; if a few find service "cranky", others compare it to "being served by your grandmother", who can "make you feel guilty if you want only one of anything."

Murray's House of Prime Kosher Beef 🚲 ▭ ⌿ | – | – | – | M |
507 Grand St. (E. B'way), 212-254-0180
For over 20 years, this Lower East Side butcher shop and market has been a source of reasonably priced kosher products, including deli meats and sausages; fresh produce is also on hand for sandwich dressing.

NEUCHATEL CHOCOLATES 🚲 ▭ | 27 | 24 | 24 | E |
60 Wall St. (bet. Pearl & William Sts.), 212-480-3766
www.neuchatelchocolates.com
◼ "Scrumptious truffles" (20 different kinds) are the bonbons of choice at this Wall Street Swiss "chocolate sleeper" where "expensive" prices are not an issue for the well-heeled clientele.

Neuman & Bogdonoff | 23 | 22 | 21 | E |
173 Chrystie St. (bet. Delancey & Rivington Sts.), 212-228-2444
www.caterernyc.com
◪ This full-service caterer can whip up any kind of menu for virtually any kind of event – private or corporate, small or large; fans salute its "very good food" and "cooperative" service ("they were great in a last-minute emergency"), but a few critics feel it's "slipped" and can be "hit-or-miss."

Shopping

New York Wine Exchange 🚴 📧 | – | – | – | E |
9 Beaver St. (bet. Broad St. & B'way), 212-422-2222
It carries a variety of wines from around the world, but this Wall Street–area store specializes in California Chardonnay and Cabernet Sauvignon; the location makes it convenient for quick post-work purchases or corporate gifts.

Ocean Seafood 🚴🚫 ▽ | 21 | 19 | 19 | M |
19-21 Henry St. (bet. Catherine & Market Sts.), 212-227-3067
■ "Big portions" of "number-one quality" seafood are sold retail in the front section of this large wholesale operation on an out-of-the-way Chinatown block; the selection is small and the atmosphere rough around the edges, but surveyors report that what the shop does carry "always hits the spot."

Olive's 🚴 | 24 | 18 | 17 | M |
120 Prince St. (bet. Greene & Wooster Sts.), 212-941-0111
◪ A "petite", "quintessential SoHo take-out shop" with "tasty" sandwiches, soups, salads and store-baked sweets so good that "no day that starts with one of their morning buns can be bad"; a few outvoted critics find it "nothing exceptional" and complain of "small portions."

Once Upon A Tart 🚴 📧 | 25 | 21 | 21 | M |
135 Sullivan St. (bet. Houston & Prince Sts.), 212-387-8869
■ Sweet and savory tarts that "melt away anxiety", "the best scones ever", "first-rate muffins" and cutting-edge sandwiches are the stock-in-trade of this "charming" SoHo bakery/cafe, a "fabulous" neighborhood retreat for "yum, yum" snacks and "great people-watching."

Paragon | 22 | 22 | 16 | M |
256 Bowery (bet. Houston & Prince Sts.), 212-226-0954
■ Though primarily a wholesale restaurant supplier, this Bowery shop also sells to the public, offering a "large selection" of "wonderful cookware" and tableware, from glasses and china to juicers, food processors, microwaves and more; overall, fans consider it "worth the price they ask."

Pepe Rosso 🚴🚫 ▽ | 22 | 19 | 21 | I |
149 Sullivan St. (bet. Houston & Prince Sts.), 212-677-4555
■ "Homestyle Italian" pastas and "can't-miss sandwiches" make for "very good" takeout at this original SoHo location of the all-over-town chainlet; with "fair prices", "friendly" service and long hours, it's "a gift to the neighborhood."

Petite Abeille 🚴 | 24 | 19 | 20 | M |
134 W. Broadway (Duane St.), 212-791-1360
■ "Belgian goodness" to go can be enjoyed via this "perky" TriBeCa link of a Downtown chainlet offering "awesome waffles", "flavorful beef stew", primo mussels and other "tasty treats"; if the selection is somewhat "limited", at least what's offered comes at an "honest price."

www.zagat.com 117

Shopping

| | Q | V | S | C |

PIEMONTE RAVIOLI   26 | 24 | 22 | I
190 Grand St. (Mulberry St.), 212-226-0475
■ An "endangered species", this Little Italy "classic" offers "old-fashioned charm" along with a "solid range" of ravioli and other "excellent", "inexpensive" fresh and dried items; some find the more "exotic" offerings "variable", but most judge it "wonderful" all-around.

PORTO RICO IMPORTING CO.   27 | 27 | 22 | I
107 Thompson St. (bet. Prince & Spring Sts.), 212-966-5758
www.portorico.com
■ Surveyors rhapsodize about the "awesome" coffees and teas at this SoHo branch of the small but significant Downtown chain where the "aroma is addicting" and they offer "more varieties than Brazil"; the "body-pierced young staff" is "savvy" and usually "helpful" (though watch out for occasional "attitude"), and many feel the "amazing prices" justify the "long lines"; devotees know it as "the city's best source for serious coffee drinkers."

Ravioli Store   25 | 24 | 23 | M
75 Sullivan St. (bet. Broome & Spring Sts.), 212-925-1737
www.raviolistore.com
■ "Wonderful variety" keeps things interesting at this SoHo store featuring "delicate, inventive" ravioli with "ingenious" fillings (lobster with scallop mousse, black beans with Jack cheese in blue corn pasta), as well as fresh pasta, gnocchi and more; if some find it "a little pricey", connoisseurs consider it a "good value."

Robert Swingle Distinctive Catering   ▽ 26 | 22 | 21 | E
159 E. Houston (bet. Allen & Aldridge), 212-353-8848
■ The in-house caterer for the Asia Society and Christie's, among other companies, this Lower East Side full-service firm handles events of any size, providing a "great selection" of Eclectic fare at "reasonable" (for the quality) prices; recently, it launched Swingle Express, which provides simpler fare for office breakfast, lunch or dinner meetings.

Ron Ben-Israel Cakes   – | – | – | E
42 Greene St., 5th fl. (bet. Broome & Grand Sts.), 212-625-3369
www.weddingcakes.com
Ron Ben-Israel uses a classic French genoise cake (light, not too sweet, yet intensely flavored) as the base for his 'couture' wedding and special-occasion creations; he will decorate them to match anything from the bridal gown to the venue's wallpaper, and rest assured that you can have your cake and eat it too, since nothing is used that's not edible – particularly amazing are his incredibly lifelike sugar flowers.

Shopping | Q | V | S | C |

Ruben's Empanadas 🚴 ⌀ | 21 | 20 | 20 | I |
505 Broome St. (W. B'way), 212-334-3351
15 Bridge St. (bet. Broad & Whitehall Sts.), 212-509-3825
South Street Seaport, 64 Fulton St., 212-962-5330

■ "As good for the taste as they are bad for the waist" say fans of the "authentic" South American empanadas turned out by this Downtown minichain; offered in savory and sweet versions, they're ideal "for a quick bite" and make "great party food"; there's also a limited selection of soups, including black bean and "good gazpacho" in the summer.

RUSS & DAUGHTERS 📄 | 27 | 26 | 24 | M |
179 E. Houston St. (bet. Allen & Orchard Sts.), 212-475-4880, 800-787-7229
www.russanddaughters.com

■ A "golden oldie" on the Lower East Side where the "faithful line up on weekends", this "Jewish jewel" "can't be beat for smoked fish" – "superb lox", "sable like velvet" and more; it also boasts "old-world service" from a "friendly staff that knows its stuff", so even if it's "a bit of a schlep", it's "worth the trip" for a "walk down memory lane."

Slavin, M. & Sons, Ltd. 🚴 📄 | 25 | 24 | 21 | M |
106 South St. (bet. Beekman St. & Peck Slip), 212-233-4522
www.mslavin.com

■ Shop like a restaurateur at one of the city's big Downtown wholesalers, where the selection is "truly phenomenal" (more than 50 varieties of seafood are usually available) and most say both the "quality and prices" are "refreshing"; the early-morning hours (call first for exact opening and closing times) aren't conducive to easy marketing, so insiders recommend it for large orders placed by phone.

Snack ⌀ | – | – | – | M |
105 Thompson St. (bet. Prince & Spring Sts.), 212-925-1040

It's all Greek to chef-owner Elias Varkoutas, whose small SoHo eat-in/take-out place offers a mainly vegetarian menu including traditional savory pastries, stuffed vegetables and spreads, plus olives, toasts, soaps and other specialty items; Elias knows his stuff, and it's obvious where he learned it once you taste the marvelous moussaka with mushrooms that his mom makes.

SoHo Wines & Spirits 🚴 | 24 | 22 | 22 | M |
461 W. Broadway (bet. Houston & Prince Sts.), 212-777-4332
www.sohowines.com

■ "A SoHo institution before the galleries and boutiques" arrived, this rather plain, modest-sized store doesn't have the glitz of its West Broadway neighbors, but locals like its "decent" selection (including some "offbeat" choices and a notable sampling of single-malt scotches), "personal service" and generally "reasonable prices" for the area.

Shopping | Q V S C

Sosa Borella ⚲ ▽ 24 | 21 | 26 | M
460 Greenwich St. (bet. Desbrosses & Watts Sts.), 212-431-5093
■ Tucked away in TriBeCa, this Argentine restaurant with Italian accents is making a name for itself as a "terrific" take-out option thanks to a large choice of "well-prepared, innovative" sandwiches and salads at lunch, plus hearty PM fare such as homemade ravioli and fettuccine or the *parrillada,* a South American mixed grill; prices are moderate and service couldn't be friendlier.

Spring Street Bakery – | – | – | M
30 Spring St. (Mott St.), 917-237-1901
Owned by a young Thai chef who trained at Troigros in France and in some of NYC's most revered kitchens (Le Cirque, La Côte Basque), this popular new bakery anchoring a corner of Little Italy offers a slice of Americana via eye-widening apple pie, real-deal doughnuts, red velvet cake, banana pudding and cookies in glass jars; omelets, salads and sandwiches are also available, as are those neighborhood fixtures, tiramisu and cannolis.

Streit Matzoh Co. ⌀ 23 | 18 | 18 | I
150 Rivington St. (bet. Clinton & Suffolk Sts.), 212-475-7000
www.streitsmatzos.com
◪ While "it's not Passover without Streit's egg matzo", this "old-fashioned factory" on the Lower East Side also sells other varieties, including lightly salted, unsalted, moonstrip (onion poppy) and whole wheat, as well as farfel and matzo meal; admit it, "once a year you need 'em."

SULLIVAN STREET BAKERY ⌀ 27 | 22 | 23 | M
73 Sullivan St. (bet. Broome & Spring Sts.), 212-334-9435
■ "A true artist" in keeping with his SoHo base, baker Jim Leahy has long studied "*molto tradizionale*" recipes, so he now "has the patent on authentic Italian breads", including "to-die-for *pane pugliese*" and "legendary ciabatta"; "serious breadheads" trek to this "unassuming location" for the "excellent raisin walnut" loaf, "pizza bianca that rings the bell" and biscotti too.

SYLVIA WEINSTOCK CAKES, LTD. ⚲⌀ 27 | 26 | 26 | VE
273 Church St. (bet. Franklin & White Sts.), 212-925-6698
By delivery only
www.sylviaweinstockcakes.com
■ Couples waffling about whether to tie the knot may find the "breathtaking" custom wedding cakes produced by this specialty baker "worth getting married for"; the "beautiful, complex" and "so pricey" designs are also showstoppers for birthdays, bar mitzvahs, etc., and while the "queen of wedding cakes" caters to a well-heeled clientele, surveyors report that she "treats all customers the same."

Shopping

| | Q | V | S | C |

Tai Pan Bakery ⌿ | – | – | – | I |
194 Canal St. (Mott St.), 212-732-2222
www.taipan-bakery.com
You'll have to fight crowds at this no-frills Chinese bakery, but it's worth the effort for freshly baked pastries ranging from savory and sweet buns to rice cakes and sesame balls; the selection is wide and the prices are right.

Taylor's ⌿ | 24 | 22 | 20 | M |
156 Chambers St. (bet. Greenwich St. & W. B'way), 212-378-3401
■ "Gooey gunky sweets of childhood", such as "monster"-size "amazing Rice Krispie treats", "wonderful sticky buns" and "first-rate brownies", are the specialty of this TriBeCa branch of the Downtown chain that's a "grunge alternative to Starbucks", complete with staff that some find "more focused on their noserings" than the customers; P.S. "if you're on a diet, don't even go near their window."

TEN REN TEA AND GINSENG CO. | 27 | 27 | 22 | M |
75 Mott St. (bet. Bayard & Canal Sts.), 212-349-1937
www.tenren.com
■ "An excellent source for top-quality teas" is the take on this Chinatown "mecca" where "special teas are beautifully displayed"; the huge array includes "super green teas" and "any herbal type you want" in a wide range of prices, and while the "lovely staff tells you everything", if you "go with a local, it's an education in itself"; teapots and related paraphernalia also make for "interesting shopping."

TriBakery 🚲 | 24 | 21 | 21 | M |
186 Franklin St. (bet. Greenwich & Hudson Sts.), 212-431-1114
■ While it formerly shared space with the defunct Italian restaurant Zeppole, this wholesale/retail bakery continues on as a supplier to Drew Nieporent's other ventures around the city; it's also a "neighborhood lifesaver" for "beautifully displayed" breads including a "superlative pan rustique", "outstanding olive bread" and awesome torpedo-shaped pretzel rolls, as well as soups, salads and sandwiches.

Tribeca Wine Merchants | – | – | – | E |
40 Hudson St. (bet. Thomas & Duane Sts.), 212-393-1400
Oenophiles may find themselves inventing occasions to visit this new upscale TriBeCa shop, because its elegant cherry wood–appointed interior is as inviting as its small, eclectic selection of wines; a glass-enclosed back room houses fine and rare vintages, which carry correspondingly rarefied price tags, but the bottles out front include many choices under $20.

Umanoff & Parsons 🚲 | 25 | 22 | 21 | M |
467 Greenwich St. (bet. Desbrosses & Watts Sts.), 212-219-2240
www.umanoffparsons.com
■ "Consistency, thy name is Umanoff (or Parsons)" declare pleased patrons of this "high-quality" TribeCa bakery that

Shopping

primarily supplies restaurants and gourmet food stores, but also offers its "fabulous chocolate mud cake", "oh my" three-berry pie, "best" apple brown betty and other all-natural goodies for retail sale; customers enter directly into the company's baking facility (there's no actual store), meaning the fragrant aromas alone are "worth the trip."

Vesuvio Bakery ⊅   23 | 19 | 21 | I
160 Prince St. (bet. Thompson St. & W. B'way), 212-925-8248
■ "Take home the pepper biscuits and open a bottle of wine" advise fans of this "charming", often photographed SoHo "landmark"; despite a "very limited selection" of Italian breads, it's "not to be missed", "if just for the friendly longtime owner" Anthony Dapolito.

Vine   – | – | – | M
25 Broad St. (Exchange Pl.), 212-344-8463
www.vinefood.com
Next to the restaurant of the same name, this market/prepared foods shop aims to be the every-meal source for Wall Street area office workers and locals (it's in The Exchange, a huge residential building); besides an ever-changing array of take-out fare – some 30 dishes daily – and pastries, it stocks gourmet grocery items like artisan cheeses and breads, and also provides catering services both off-premises and for delivery.

Vintage New York   – | – | – | M
482 Broome St. (bet. Wooster & Greene Sts.), 212-226-9463
www.vintagenewyork.com
It's the only wine shop in NYC that's open on Sunday (legal because it's owned by a vineyard, New Paltz's Rivendell), and that's not the only thing that sets this SoHo store apart from the pack: it carries wines from NY State exclusively, and all 200 or so labels can be sampled at an attractive back tasting counter before purchase; it also stocks NY cheeses, oils and other gourmet items, has a rentable party space downstairs and regularly hosts lectures and classes on food and wine.

Yonah Schimmell's Knishes   22 | 19 | 17 | I
137 E. Houston St. (bet. 1st & 2nd Aves.), 212-477-2858
■ Take a "trip back in time" to when "a knish was a real knish" at this Lower East Side "landmark" that prepares "moist, plump, tasty" versions with kasha, meat, potato, cabbage and other "sit-in-your-belly-forever" fillings; sure, a jaded contingent yawns "nothing to rave about" and tidiness has never been the store's strong suit, but a salivating majority says "I can taste them now."

Shopping Indexes

**CATEGORIES
LOCATIONS**

Shopping Category Index

CATEGORIES

Bagels and Bialys
Kossar's Bialys

Baked Goods
Baked Ideas
Balthazar Bakery
Barocco
Bijoux Doux
Caffé Roma Pastry
Ceci-Cela
Connecticut Muffin
Dean & DeLuca
Doughnut Plant
Duane Park Patisserie
Eileen's Cheesecake
Ferrara Cafe
Gertel's Bake Shop
Houghtaling Mousse Pie
Le Pain Quotidien
Lung Moon Bakery
Maria's Bakery
Moishe's Kosher
Once Upon a Tart
Ron Ben-Israel Cakes
Spring Street Bakery
Streit Matzoh Co.
Sullivan St. Bakery
Sylvia Weinstock Cakes
Tai Pan Bakery
Taylor's
TriBakery
Umanoff & Parsons
Vesuvio Bakery
Vine

Candy & Nuts
Aji Ichiban
Bazzini, A.L.
Dean & DeLuca
Economy Candy
Godiva Chocolatier
Kadouri & Sons
Leonidas
Neuchatel Chocolates

Caterers and Event Planners
Barrraud Caterers
Bridgewaters
Charlotte's Catering
Dean & DeLuca
Food in Motion
Great Performances
Mangia
Manna
Neuman & Bogdonoff
Robert Swingle Catering
Vine

Caviar & Smoked Fish
Dean & DeLuca
Russ & Daughters

Cheese & Dairy
Alleva Dairy
Dean & DeLuca
DiPalo Dairy
Gourmet Garage
Joe's Dairy
Vintage New York

Coffee & Tea
Bell Bates Natural Market
Dean & DeLuca
Kelley & Ping
Porto Rico Importing
Ten Ren Tea

Cookware & Supplies
Bari Restaurant Equipment
Broadway Panhandler
Dean & DeLuca
Hung Chong Import
Matas Restaurant Supply
Paragon

Fish
Centre Seafood
Dean & DeLuca
Gourmet Garage
G.S. Food Market
Hai Thanh Seafood
Ocean Seafood
Slavin, M. & Sons

Flowers
Blue Water Flowers
Flowers of the World

Food Specialty Shops
Chung Chou City
Dean & DeLuca
Fong Inn Too

Shopping Category Index

Gourmet Garage
Guss' Pickles
Hong Kong Supermarket
Italian Food Center
Kam Kuo Food Corp.
Kam Man

Health & Natural Foods
Bell Bates Natural Food
Healthy Pleasures
Herban Kitchen

Ice Cream & Frozen Yogurt
Baskin-Robbins
Chinatown Ice Cream
Ciao Bella Gelato
Häagen Dazs

Meat & Poultry
Bayard St. Meat Market
Catherine St. Meat Market
Dean & DeLuca
Grand St. Sausages
Murray's House of Beef

Pastas
Dean & DeLuca
DiPalo Dairy
Piemonte Ravioli
Ravioli Store

Prepared Foods
Barocco
Columbine
Daily Soup
Dean & DeLuca
Deb's
Donald Sacks
Kam Man
Le Pain Quotidien
Little Place
Mangia
Olive's
Pepe Rosso
Petite Abeille
Ruben's Empanadas
Snack
Sosa Borella
Vine
Yonah Schimmell's
Vine

Produce
Dean & DeLuca
Gourmet Garage
Healthy Pleasures

Wines & Liquor
Famous Wines
New York Wine Exchange
SoHo Wines
Tribeca Wine Merchants
Vintage New York

Shopping Location Index

LOCATIONS

Chinatown
Aji Ichiban
Bayard St. Meat
Catherine St. Meat
Centre Seafood
Chinatown Ice Cream
Chung Chou City
Fong Inn Too
Häagen Dazs
Hai Thanh Seafood
Hong Kong Supermarket
Hung Chong Import
Kam Kuo Food Corp.
Kam Man
Lung Moon Bakery
Maria's Bakery
Ocean Seafood
Tai Pan Bakery
Ten Ren Tea

Financial District
Bridgewater's
Charlotte's Catering
Daily Soup
Donald Sacks
Famous Wines
Flowers of the World
Food in Motion
Godiva Chocolatier
Häagen Dazs
Leonidas
Mangia
Neuchatel Chocolates
New York Wine Exch.
Ruben's Empanadas
Slavin, M. & Sons
Vine

Little Italy
Alleva Dairy
Bari Rest. Equipment
Barraud Caterers
Bijoux Doux
Caffé Roma Pastry
Ceci-Cela
Ciao Bello Gelato
Connecticut Muffin
DiPalo Dairy
Eileen's Cheesecake
Ferrara Cafe
Grand St. Sausages
Houghtaling Mousse Pie
Italian Food Center
Matas Rest. Supply
Paragon
Piemonte Ravioli
Spring St. Bakery

Lower East Side
Baskin-Robbins
Doughnut Plant
Economy Candy
Gertel's Bake Shop
G.S. Food Market
Guss' Pickles
Kadouri & Sons
Kossar's Bialys
Moishe's Kosher
Murray's House of Beef
Neuman & Bogdonoff
Robert Swingle
Russ & Daughters
Streit Matzoh Co.
Yonah Schimmell's

SoHo
Baked Ideas
Balthazer Bakery
Blue Water Flowers
Broadway Panhandler
Dean & DeLuca
Deb's
Gourmet Garage
Great Performances
Healthy Pleasures
Herban Kitchen
Joe's Dairy
Kelley & Ping
Le Pain Quotidien
Olive's
Once Upon A Tart
Pepe Rosso
Porto Rico Importing
Ravioli Store

Shopping Location Index

Ron Ben-Israel Cakes
Ruben's Empanada's
Snack
SoHo Wines
Sullivan St. Bakery
Vesuvio Bakery
Vintage New York

TriBeCa
Barocco
Bazzini , A.L.
Bell Bates Natural Mkt.
Columbine
Duane Park Patisserie
Little Place
Manna
Petite Abeille
Sosa Borella
Sylvia Weinstock Cakes
Taylor's
TriBakery
Tribeca Wine Merchants
Umanoff & Parsons

Hotels

Hotel Map

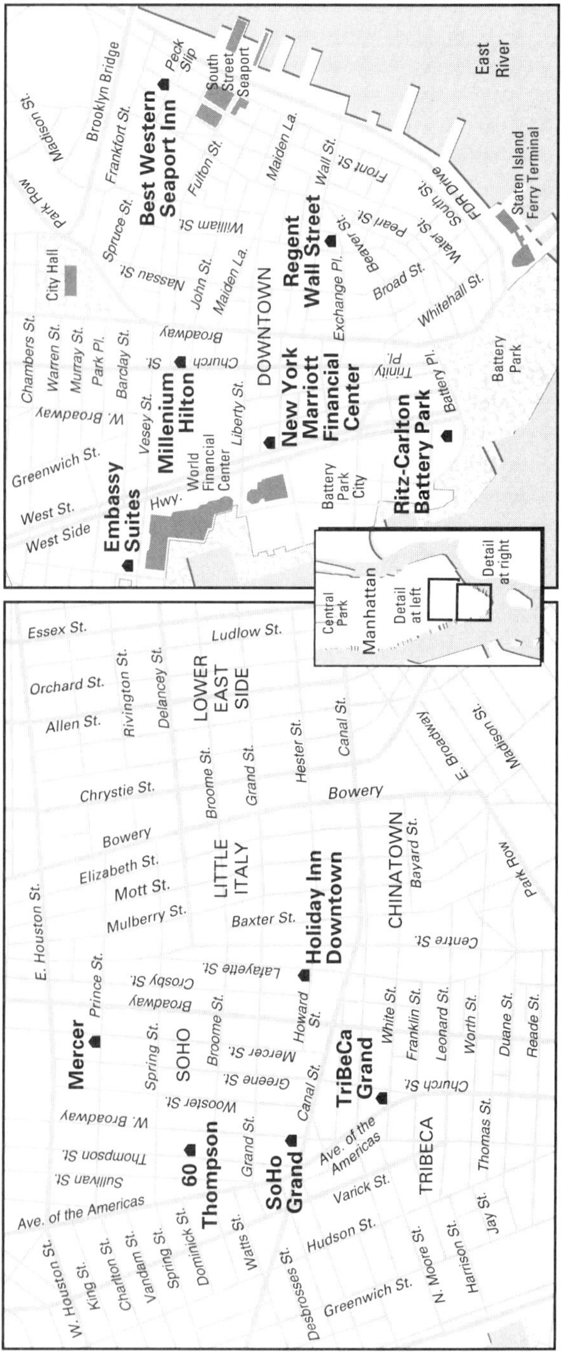

Key to Ratings/Symbols

Name, Address, Phone & Fax Nos., Web Site, Rooms

Zagat Ratings

R	S	D	P	$
▽ 16	5	4	22	$150

TIM & NINA'S INN

4 Columbus Circle; 212-977-6000; fax 212-977-9760; 800-977-9000; www.zagat.com; 20 rooms (2 suites)

◪ Despite "dazzling views" of Central Park and "lovely public spaces", surveyors are split over this "miniscule" "mini-priced" Midtown boutique hotel; fans tout its "handy location", but critics knock "rooms too small to change your mind", dining at Chez Z that's "outshone by the corner hot dog stand" and a staff that "makes Attica guards seem agreeable."

Review, with surveyors' comments in quotes

- The total number of rooms per property is followed by the number of suites as a subset, e.g. 20 rooms (2 suites).

- **Ratings:** Rooms, Service, Dining and Public Spaces/Facilities of Hotels are rated on a scale of **0** to **30** as follows:

R Rooms	S Service	D Dining	P Public Spaces/Facilities
16	5	4	22

10–15 fair to good
16–19 good to very good
20–25 very good to excellent
26–30 extraordinary to perfection
▽ low response/less reliable

- The **Cost ($)** column reflects surveyors' recollection of what they paid for a double room for one night and *should be used only as a benchmark,* since it does not reflect subsequent price increases, and rates vary by season and even time of week.

- These symbols show if comments are uniform ◼ or mixed ◪.

- A place listed without ratings is a **write-in** or **newcomer.** In these cases, cost is indicated as follows:

I	Inexpensive, below $150	E	Expensive, $250–$349
M	Moderate, $150–$249	VE	Very Expensive, $350 & up

Hotels

| R | S | D | P | $ |

Best Western Seaport Inn — | — | — | — | M
33 Peck Slip; 212-766-6600; fax 212-766-6615; 800-528-1234; www.bestwestern.com; 72 rooms
Its convenient location near the Seaport and the Financial District makes this charming restoration of a 19th-century building ideal for tourists or business travelers; added attractions include terraces with views of the Brooklyn Bridge and proximity to pierside restaurants.

Embassy Suites Hotel — | — | — | — | VE
102 North End Ave.; 212-945-0100; fax 212-945-3012; 800-362-2779; www.embassysuites.com; 463 suites
This 15-story Downtown hotel presents a roomier-than-usual New York option, with suites ranging from 450 to 800 square feet (all with high-speed Internet access) atop a 16-screen cinema and tens of thousands more feet of retail space; in contrast to all the commercialism is an A-list of specially commissioned art works from Sol LeWitt and Pat Steier, among others; N.B. located just north of the World Financial Center, the hotel was **closed at press time**.

Holiday Inn Downtown — | — | — | — | I
138 Lafayette St.; 212-966-8898; fax 212-966-3933; 800-465-4329; www.holiday-inn.com; 227 rooms (12 suites)
Set at the crossroads of SoHo, Chinatown and Little Italy, a bustling area filled with shops, galleries and restaurants, this recently renovated chain link blends modern amenities with Asian-influenced decor; its Pan-Asian restaurant, Pacifica, preserves the East-meets-West motif.

Mercer, The 26 | 24 | 26 | 24 | $350
147 Mercer St.; 212-966-6060; fax 212-965-3838; 888-918-6060; www.mercerhotel.com; 75 rooms (6 suites)
◪ The "calm, cool and sexy" sophomore SoHo hotel from André Balazs renders some fans speechless ("too hip for words") with its "stylish" postmodern decor, "celeb-watching in the lobby" and "small" but loftlike rooms ("very New York"); guests seem to revel in "wanna-be cool" service that's "attentive" but "snooty" and advise "don't miss Mercer Kitchen" for "wonderful" New American food (and room service); "bothersome street noise" irks light sleepers at this "prime locale."

Millenium Hilton 23 | 22 | 20 | 21 | $243
55 Church St.; 212-693-2001; fax 212-571-2316; 800-774-1500; www.hilton.com; 561 rooms (102 suites)
■ Directly opposite the WTC site, this "sleek" Financial District high-rise was damaged by the September 11 attacks and remains **closed at press time**; when, and if, it reopens, the hotel will offer "fabulous" river views (and an even more dramatic overlook of Ground Zero), along with all the necessary business amenities (e.g. dataports, two-line speaker phones) as well as after-hours recreation with a "decent gym" and "chic" bar scene.

Hotels | R | S | D | P | $

New York Marriott Financial Center   — | — | — | — | M
85 West St.; 212-546-8801; 800-228-9290; 504 rooms (13 suites)
This chain link was designed to cater to the business traveler with its Financial District location, terrific views of the Statue of Liberty, amenities such as high-speed Internet access, a health club, indoor pool, plus the excellent Roy's New York restaurant (an outpost of chef Yamaguchi's Pan-Asian empire); however, being located just south of the WTC, it remains **closed at press time.**

Regent Wall Street   — | — | — | — | VE
55 Wall St.; 212-845-8600; fax 212-845-8601; 800-545-4000; www.regenthotels.com; 144 rooms (47 suites)
Behind the Greek Revival columns that testify to the original purpose (NY Merchants Exchange) of this Wall Street landmark emerges a new luxury boutique property, which looks to the future while embracing the past; rooms are equipped with the digital amenities 21st-century business types have come to expect (DVDs, CDs, fax/printer/copy machines), and the marble-and-gilt ballroom is grand enough to fete any grand event.

Ritz-Carlton Battery Park   — | — | — | — | VE
2 West St.; 212-344-0800; fax 212-344-3804; 800-241-3333; www.ritzcarlton.com; 298 rooms (44 suites)
Delayed by the September 11 attacks, the opening of this luxury chain's newest Manhattan outpost is now scheduled for early 2002; along with the usual high-end amenities comes a convenient Wall Street–area address for business travelers as well as a relaxing Battery Park setting and sweeping harbor vistas for leisure seekers (many rooms come equipped with telescopes to further enhance the views); dining options will include a lobby-level restaurant with both indoor and outdoor seating, and a 14th-floor bar with a rooftop terrace.

60 Thompson   — | — | — | — | VE
60 Thompson St.; 212-431-0400; fax 212-431-0200; 877-431-0400; www.60thompson.com; 100 rooms (10 suites)
The rooftop bar and penthouse loft command panoramic views of SoHo at this newcomer sporting a mid-century style carefully cultivated by Aero Studio designer Thomas O'Brien; all rooms sport leather or suede wall paneling, rich wood furnishings, Frette linens and abstract photographs, and the high-style Thom restaurant offers a Pan-Asian menu from the creative talents behind Bond Street and Indochine.

SoHo Grand Hotel   22 | 23 | 23 | 24 | $297
310 W. Broadway; 212-965-3000; fax 212-965-3200; 800-965-3000; www.sohogrand.com; 369 rooms (4 suites)
◼ "Hip, hip, hooray!" applaud "people-watchers" at this "swank" "eyeful" in a "chic neighborhood"; accolades abound for the stainless steel "high design", the "trendy-

Hotels   R | S | D | P | $

with-manners" staff and "surprising quality" of its newly revamped restaurant, the Gallery, but many bemoan "smaller than small" rooms ("should be called SoHo Closet"), even if they do come with Kiehl's toiletries; "more for the movie star than the CEO", this "in place" lures the "young hipsters and European travelers" to its "outstanding" bar.

TriBeCa Grand Hotel   – | – | – | – | VE
2 Sixth Ave.; 212-519-6600; fax 212-519-6700; 877-519-6600; www.tribecagrand.com; 203 rooms (7 suites)
This gritty-yet-glam neighborhood of artist studios and millionaire lofts got its own luxury hotel in May 2000; while Internet drones tap away on wireless keyboards glued to Herman Miller chairs inside minimalist rooms, indie-film types rent the on-site Screening Room and the rest of the crowd heads for Church Lounge, the theatrically lit living room, where meeting, lounging and dining mix in one heady cocktail.

Attractions

Attractions Map

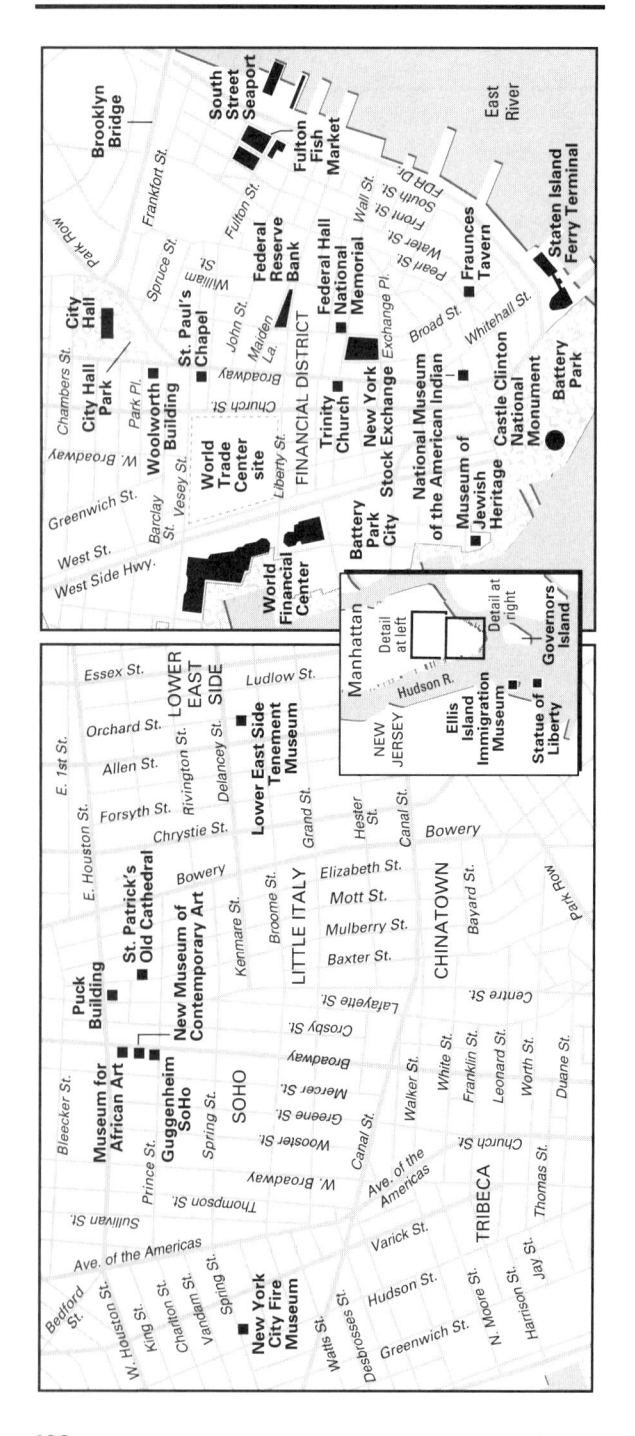

Attractions

Battery Park
Southwest tip of Manhattan
This generous patch of green flanks a fine promenade that hugs the Hudson, wending southeast from Castle Clinton down to the Staten Island Ferry terminal; it's a prime destination for picture-postcard views of Ellis and Governors Islands, Jersey City and that lovely lady in the harbor.

Battery Park City
From Chambers St. to Pier A, West St. to the Hudson River
Built on landfill excavated when the WTC was constructed, this residential community overlooks the Hudson River and houses upward of 9,000 people; it's anchored by the temporarily vacated World Financial Center, with an adjacent marina that pleases both pedestrians and diners.

Brooklyn Bridge
Entrance opposite City Hall
As much of an engineering marvel today as when it was completed in 1883, this elegant stone-and-steel suspension bridge designed by John Roebling spans the East River from Brooklyn Heights to Lower Manhattan; strollers and cyclists have their own elevated pathway that offers priceless skyline views.

Castle Clinton National Monument
Battery Park (bet. State St. & Battery Pl.), 212-344-7220
A circular fort constructed in 1811 to defend the city from attack, then renamed Castle Garden for a time and used for popular entertainment (Jenny Lind sang there); after the Civil War, it served as the official entry point in Manhattan for thousands of immigrants, and today it houses ticket booths for Ellis Island and the Statue of Liberty.

CHINATOWN
From Hester to Pearl Sts., the Bowery to Broadway
The bustling hub of the city's Chinese community lures shoppers with exotic, bargain-priced produce, fish, clothing and housewares (and also offers culinary adventures via dim sum, Peking duck or afternoon tea at a host of excellent restaurants); over the years, the area has become more ethnically diverse, with a growing non-Chinese population.

CITY HALL AND CITY HALL PARK
Between Broadway & Park Row, south of Chambers St.
Built in 1812, NYC's municipal center houses the mayor's office, the City Council Chamber, a number of museum-quality public spaces and steps that are a familiar site for politicians' press conferences; though currently closed except for official use, it's the site for government fetes and has hosted celebrations for everything from Charles Lindbergh's transatlantic flight to Neil Armstrong's walk on the moon; there's a recently refurbished park to the south anchored by a sprightly fountain.

www.zagat.com   137

Attractions

ELLIS ISLAND
Ticket booth at Battery Park (bet. State St. & Battery Pl.), 212-363-8340
From 1892 until 1924, this slip of land in the Hudson was a processing depot for millions of immigrants coming to the U.S., and its iconic Main Building, transformed into a museum and interactive learning center, now welcomes visitors; other former hospital and quarantine facilities on the island remain abandoned but still serve as ghostly reminders of the immigrants' experience; **N.B. closed at press time.**

FEDERAL HALL NATIONAL MEMORIAL
26 Wall St. (Nassau St.), 212-825-6888
The storied corner of Nassau and Wall Streets was the site of the NY colony's government and briefly functioned as the country's first capitol (George Washington was inaugurated here); over the years, it housed the U.S. Custom House, among other government offices, and currently features exhibits pertaining to the city and its history.

Federal Reserve Bank of New York
33 Liberty St. (bet. Nassau & William Sts.), 212-720-6130
Housed in a hulking Italian Renaissance–style building, the NY Fed sees the most activity of any Federal Reserve bank and also stockpiles a staggering amount of securities and gold bullion in tightly secured subterranean vaults; public access is by guided tour only, which requires an advance reservation; **N.B. closed at press time.**

FINANCIAL DISTRICT
South of Chambers St.
The portion of lower Manhattan where scrappy 17th-century colonists first set up shop now serves as the de facto control center for American capitalism; extending from Chambers Street south to Battery Park, this area is home to Wall Street, the New York and American Stock Exchanges, numerous banks and countless other businesses, as well as some of the city's oldest historic monuments and buildings.

Fraunces Tavern Museum
54 Pearl St. (Broad St.), 212-425-1778
This refurbished Colonial-era private home turned tavern is famed as the site where George Washington bid farewell to his troops at the close of the American Revolution; there's a restaurant and bar on the ground floor, while upstairs is a museum detailing 18th-century city history.

Fulton Fish Market
Fulton St. (South St.), 212-748-8786 for information on tours
Chefs, grocers and night owls with a piscatory bent mingle and haggle at this wholesale fish market, a vibrant remnant of the seaport's 19th-century maritime commerce; open

Attractions

Monday–Friday from 11 PM–6 AM, it's fun for a visit and a nosh at one of the nearby all-night eateries.

Governors Island
Southeast tip of Manhattan
Strategically situated between Brooklyn and the southern tip of Manhattan, this lovely, campus-like island, with its Fort Jay and Castle Williams citadels still intact, was used to defend Manhattan during the Revolution and the War of 1812 and later served as a Coast Guard base; currently off-limits to the public, its fate is being discussed by the State and Congress.

Guggenheim SoHo
575 Broadway (Prince St.), 212-423-3500
An offshoot of Uptown's Guggenheim Museum, this scaled-down branch offers a variety of exhibits in art-centric SoHo; given the consumer-friendly environs, it's no surprise that the gift shop is almost as large as the gallery space.

LITTLE ITALY
From Houston to Canal Sts., the Bowery to Lafayette St.
Italian immigrants settled in this neighborhood, starting in the 19th century; roughly bounded by Houston, Canal and Lafayette Streets and the Bowery, its heart is Mulberry Street, site of the annual San Gennaro festival; while its perimeters have been constricting in recent years due to the ever-growing Chinatown, it remains a lively destination for a pasta supper or a traditional pastry – and its *Godfather*-esque vibe adds vicarious frisson.

Lower East Side
From Houston St. to the Manhattan Bridge, the East River to the Bowery
A handful of kosher food shops and Hebrew signs for long-defunct businesses recall the days when this area, bounded by Houston and Canal Streets east of the Bowery, was the arrival point for much of NY's Jewish population; more recently, it has become a fashionable nexus for starving artists and night owls, with the result that discount clothiers now lie cheek by jowl with hip boutiques and watering holes.

Lower East Side Tenement Museum
90 Orchard St. (Broome St.), 212-431-0233
An evocative Lower East Side museum that offers a tour of an 1863 tenement building, untouched since the '30s, that housed over 7,000 immigrant workers over the years; the size of a typical Manhattan studio apartment takes on new meaning after a look at these tight quarters.

Museum for African Art
593 Broadway (bet. Houston & Prince Sts.), 212-966-1313
Founded as the Center for African Art, this compact SoHo museum set in an atmospheric space designed by Maya Lin focuses on the arts and culture of the African continent.

Attractions

Museum of Jewish Heritage
18 First Pl. (Battery Pl.), 212-968-1800
Subtitled "A Living Memorial to the Holocaust", this fascinating Battery Park City museum uses its rich collection of personal objects, photographs, films and documents to convey the history of Jewish life and the legacy of the Holocaust; it's set to undergo expansion at press time.

National Museum of the American Indian
U.S. Custom House, 1 Bowling Green (State St.), 212-668-6624
The local outpost of the Smithsonian Institute's similarly named museum, set in the stately beaux arts former U.S. Custom House; in addition to an extensive collection of art and artifacts pertaining to the culture of the indigenous peoples of the Americas, there's also a splendid rotunda adorned with murals by Reginald Marsh.

New Museum of Contemporary Art
583 Broadway (bet. Houston & Prince Sts.), 212-219-1355
Reflecting its location in the heart of arty SoHo, this museum might be the MOMA of the Moby crowd; set in a former loft building, it's got its finger on the art-world pulse, showcasing up-to-the-minute multimedia works by international artists seldom seen at other venues around town.

New York City Fire Museum
278 Spring St. (bet. Hudson & Varick Sts.), 212-691-1303
A fitting place to celebrate NY's Bravest is this former firehouse in SoHo that displays an impressive collection of art, objects and equipment relating to firefighting and charts the FDNY's history through a number of devastating fires.

New York Stock Exchange
20 Broad St. (bet. Wall St. & Exchange Pl.), 212-656-5168
What began in 1792 as 22 brokers congregating around a buttonwood tree has evolved into the high-tech epicenter of the world's securities markets where, each weekday, after the ringing of the Opening Bell, thousands of trades are processed; following the September 11 attacks, the NYSE was able to reopen the following Monday, and has closed out billions of dollars worth of trades since then; **N.B. closed to visitors at press time.**

Puck Building
295 Lafayette St. (Houston St.), 212-274-8900
This handsome edifice is a gatepost of sorts to SoHo, erected in 1885 as the headquarters of *Puck,* a popular satirical magazine (its waggish namesake is rendered in two statues adorning the facade); now housing offices and party spaces, it's a popular setting for private events.

Attractions

SOHO
From Houston to Canal Sts., Lafayette St. to the Hudson River
Short for "South of Houston", SoHo is a living museum of 19th-century cast-iron architecture populated today by trendy art galleries, hotels and eateries; most of the action is concentrated on its two main thoroughfares, Broadway and West Broadway, but there's also plenty going on along its fascinating cross streets, Prince, Spring, Broome and Grand.

SOUTH STREET SEAPORT
From Pearl to South Sts., Dover St. to Schermerhorn Row, 212-699-9400
Some of NY's oldest buildings and piers, dating from the 18th century, have been preserved and remodeled into this major tourist attraction highlighted by a fleet of period vessels; unabashedly family-oriented, the area is studded with shops, restaurants and watering holes, many of which offer stunning harbor views.

Staten Island Ferry
Whitehall Terminal at the southern tip of Manhattan, 718-815-2628
This ferry shuttles commuters and tourists across five scenic miles of New York harbor between the southern tip of Manhattan and Richmond Terrace on Staten Island, passing Ellis, Governors and Liberty Islands on the way; you can't beat the price – free to pedestrians; a new Whitehall Ferry Terminal is currently in the works, along with a renovated Peter Minuet Plaza.

STATUE OF LIBERTY
Ticket booth at Battery Park (bet. State St. & Battery Pl.), 212-363-3200
Conceived to embody the amity between France and the U.S., this American icon has served as a beacon in NY harbor and a symbol of freedom since its dedication in 1886; rubberneckers take an elevator to the observation deck at its base, while the spry can scale 354 steps for the view from its crown, but bear in mind that a visit here can eat up half a day, mostly spent on lines; **N.B. closed at press time.**

St. Patrick's Old Cathedral
233 Mott St. (bet. Prince & Spring Sts.), 212-226-3984
New York's first Roman Catholic cathedral was housed in this simple church, named for the patron saint of Ireland; dedicated in 1815 and rebuilt following a fire in 1866, it became a parish church following the 1879 completion of its much grander Uptown namesake on Fifth Avenue; today, its courtyard offers some tranquility in the otherwise bustling NoLita neighborhood.

www.zagat.com

Attractions

St. Paul's Chapel
211 Broadway (bet. Fulton & Vesey Sts.), 212-602-0800
George Washington once worshipped at this 1766 Georgian chapel, the oldest surviving church in Manhattan (and an affiliate of nearby Trinity Church); although near Ground Zero, the chapel miraculously survived the September 11 attacks and has served since then as both a relief and spiritual shelter for rescue workers.

TriBeCa
From Canal to Chambers Sts., Broadway to the Hudson River
Shorthand for "Triangle Below Canal" Street, this trapezoidal slice of old NY developed in the late 19th century as a cluster of warehouses anchored by the Washington Market, the city's largest fruit and produce supplier; it lost its gritty character in the 1970s as real estate developers remade its industrial spaces into pricey residential lofts, shops and restaurants.

Trinity Church and Cemetery
Broadway at Wall St., 212-602-0872
Founded by royal grant in 1697 and twice rebuilt, this circa 1839 Anglican church is the city's best-known chapel and the oldest public building in continuous use in town; its cemetery contains the gravestones of many illustrious historical figures, among them Alexander Hamilton and Robert Fulton.

Wall Street
Between Broadway & the East River, south of Pine St.
Thanks to Hollywood and some larger-than-life real-life players, the very name of this Financial District artery conjures up visions of power suits, Midas-size piles of dough and equally spectacular losses of fortune; named for the wall that once fortified the New Amsterdam community, today it's an imposing cavern lined by such noteworthy buildings as the J.P. Morgan tower, 55 Wall and Federal Hall.

Woolworth Building
233 Broadway (bet. Barclay & Vesey Sts.)
A younger generation of skyscrapers now overshadows F.W. Woolworth's ornate tower – the tallest in the world for a time – but few can best its must-see lobby, crowned by a stunning, gold mosaic-tiled ceiling that makes for Sistine Chapel–style neck-craning.

World Financial Center
From Vesey to Albany Sts., West St. to the Hudson River
As the name suggests, this cluster of four soaring towers at the northern edge of Battery Park City is home to financial heavyweights like American Express, Merrill Lynch, Dow Jones and the New York Mercantile Exchange, as well as restaurants, shops and a Hudson-front plaza;

Attractions

its centerpiece is the spectacular Winter Garden, a soaring atrium used for both public performances and private events; damaged by the September 11 attacks, the WFC is under reconstruction but closed at press time.

WORLD TRADE CENTER SITE
From Vesey to Liberty Sts., Church to West Sts.
The enormous void left by the destruction of the Twin Towers is the most powerful reminder of the September 11 terrorist attacks; completed in 1970 under the aegis of the NY Port Authority, the buildings were symbolic of the city's role in international commerce, as well as the absolute belief that with energy and enterprise, the sky is truly the limit; as we go to press, workers and volunteers of all stripes continue to clear debris as discussions for an appropriate memorial and the eventual redevelopment of the site are underway; God bless America.

Location Indexes

Location Index

LOCATIONS

Chinatown
Aji Ichiban
Ajisen Noodle
Ba Ba Malaysian
Bayard St. Meat
Big Wong
Bo-Ky
Canton
Catherine St. Meat
Centre Seafood
Chinatown Ice Cream
Chung Chou City
Dim Sum Go Go
Evergreen Shanghai
Excellent Dumpling
Fong Inn Too
Fun
Golden Unicorn
Goody's
Grand Sichuan
Great NY Noodle Town
Häagen Dazs
Hai Thanh Seafood
Hong Kong Supermarket
Hung Chong Import
HSF
Joe's Shanghai
Kam Chueh
Kam Kuo Food Corp.
Kam Man
Lung Moon Bakery
Mandarin Court
Maria's Bakery
New Green Bo
New Pasteur
Nha Trang
Nice Restaurant
Ocean Seafood
Oriental Garden
Peking Duck House
Pho Bang
Pho Viet Huong
Ping's
Shanghai Cuisine
Sweet-n-Tart Cafe
Tai Hong Lau
Tai Pan Bakery
Ten Ren Tea
Thailand Restaurant
Triple Eight
27 Sunrise Seafood

Vegetarian Paradise
Vietnam
Winnie's
Wo Hop
Wong Kee
XO Kitchen

Financial District
American Park
Au Mandarin
Bayard's
Bayard's Blue Bar
Beckett's B/G
Blarney Stone
Bridge Cafe
Bridgewater's
Burritoville
Cabana
Charlotte's Catering
Cosi Sandwich
Daily Soup
Dakota Roadhouse
Delmonico's
Divine Bar
Donald Sacks
Edward Moran
Embassy Suites Hotel
Famous Wines
Flowers of the World
55 Wall
14 Wall St.
Food in Motion
Fraunces Tavern
Full Shilling
Gigino at Wagner Park
Godiva Chocolatier
Grill Room
Häagen Dazs
Harbour Lights
Harry's at Hanover Square
Houlihan's
Hudson River Club
Il Giglio
Jeremy's Ale House
John St. B/G
Leonidas
Lili's Noodle Shop
Little Italy
Little Place
Mangia
MarkJoseph
Mercantile Grill

Location Index

Millenium Hilton
Neuchatel Chocolates
New York Marriott Financial Ctr.
New York Wine Exchange
Orange Bear
Paris Cafe
Pizzeria Uno
Quartino
Raccoon Lodge
Regent Wall St. Hotel
Roy's NY
Ruben's Empanadas
St. Maggie's Cafe
Slavin, M. & Sons
SouthWest NY
Starbucks
St. Maggie's Cafe
T.G.I. Friday's
Vine
Wall St. Kitchen

Little Italy

Alleva Dairy
Angelo's
Bari Restaurant Equipment
Barraud Caterers
Bijoux Doux
Bistrot Margot
Bot
Botanica Bar
Cafe Colonial
Cafe Gitane
Cafe Habana
Caffe Roma Pastry
Ceci-Cela
Chibi's
Ciao Bello Gelato
Clay
Connecticut Muffin
Da Nico
DiPalo Dairy
Double Happiness
Eight Mile Creek
Eileen's Cheesecake
Ferrara
Funky Broome
Ghenet
Grand St. Sausages
Houghtaling Mousse Pie
Il Cortile
Il Fornaio
Il Palazzo
Italian Food Center
Kitchen Club

La Mela
Le Jardin
Lombardi's
M & R Bar
Matas Restaurant Supply
Mare Chiaro
MeKong
Mexican Radio
Milano's Bar
Nyonya
Onieal's
Paragon
Peasant
Pellegrino's
Pho Bang
Piemonte Ravioli
Positano
Pravda
Rialto
Rice
Sal's S.P.Q.R.
Spring Lounge
Spring Street Bakery
Sweet & Vicious
Taormina
Va Tutto!
Velvet
Vig Bar
Wyanoka

Lower East Side

AKA Cafe
Angel
Arlene Grocery
Barramundi
Barrio
Baskin-Robbins
Bereket
bOb Bar
Bowery Ballroom
Casa Mexicana
Doughnut Plant
Economy Candy
Essex Restaurant
1492 Food
Gertel's Bake Shop
Good World Bar & Grill
Grilled Cheese
G.S. Food Market
Guss' Pickles
Idlewild
Iggy's Keltic Lounge
Kadouri & Sons
Katz's Deli

www.zagat.com 147

Location Index

Kossar's Bialys
Kush
Lansky Lounge
Le Pere Pinard
Living Room
Local 138
Lolita
Lotus Cafe
Ludlow Bar
Luna Lounge
Max Fish
Meow Mix
Mercury Lounge
Milk and Honey
Mint
Moishe's Kosher
Mooza
Motor City Bar
Murray's House of Beef
Neuman & Bogdonoff
Oliva
Orchard Bar
Paladar
Pink Pony
Ratner's
Rivertown Lounge
Robert Swingle
Russ & Daughters
Sammy's Roumanian
Sapphire Lounge
71 Clinton Fresh Food
Slipper Room
Streit Matzoh Co.
Swim
SX 137
Tonic
Torch
205 Club
Welcome to the Johnsons
Whiskey Ward
Wyanoka
Yonah Schimmell's

SoHo

Alison on Dominick
Antarctica
Aquagrill
Bacco
Baked Ideas
Balthazar
Balthazar Bakery
Baluchi's
Bar 89
Barolo
Bistro Les Amis
Blue Ribbon
Blue Ribbon Sushi
Blue Water Flowers
Boom
Broadway Panhandler
Broome St. Bar
Cafe Noir
Canteen
Casa La Femme
Cendrillon
Chez Bernard
Circa Tabac
Country Cafe
Cub Room
Culture Club
Cupping Room Cafe
Cyber Cafe
Dean & DeLuca
Deb's
Denial
Diva
Don Hill's
Ear Inn
Fanelli's Cafe
Félix
Gallery, The
Gourmet Garage
Grand Bar
Great Performances
Hampton Chutney Co.
Healthy Pleasures
Herban Kitchen
Honmura An
Ideya
Il Corallo
I Tre Merli
Jean Claude
Jerry's
Joe's Dairy
Kaña
Kavehaz
Kelley & Ping
Kin Khao
La Jumelle
L'Ecole
Le Gamin
Le Pain Quotidien
Le Pescadou
Little Italy Pizza
L'Orange Bleue
Lucky Strike
L'Ulivo
Manhattan Bistro

Location Index

Merc Bar
Mercer Bar
Mercer Hotel
Mercer Kitchen
Mezzogiorno
Milady's
Ñ
Naked Lunch
Namaskaar
Nello
Novocento
NV/289
Olive's
Omen
Once Upon a Tart
Oro Blu
Pão!
Penang
Pepe Rosso
Pfiff
Porto Rico Importing
Pravda
Provence
Puck Fair
Quilty's
Raoul's
Ravioli Store
Recess
Red Bench
Ron Ben-Israel Cakes
Room, The
Ruben's Empanadas
Savore
Savoy
Scharmann's
Sirocco
60 Thompson Hotel
Snack
S.O.B.'s
Soho Grand Hotel
Soho Steak
Soho Wines
Spring St. Natural
Starbucks
Stella
Sullivan St. Bakery
Sway
Tennessee Mountain
Thom
Thom's Bar
357
Toad Hall
203 Spring St.
Veruka

Vesuvio Bakery
Vintage NY
Void
Woo Lae Oak
Zinc Bar
Zoë

TriBeCa
Acappella
Anotheroom
Arqua
Baby Doll Lounge
Barocco
Bazzini, A.L.
Bell Bates Natural Market
Bouley Bakery
Bubble Lounge
Bubby's
Capsuoto Frères
Chanterelle
Church Lounge
City Hall
Columbine
Danube
Duane Park Cafe
Duane Park Patisserie
Dylan Prime
Ecco
Edward's
El Teddy's
F.illi Ponte
Flor De Sol
Gigino
Grace
Harrison, The
Independent, The
Ivy's Bistro
Juniper Cafe
Kitchenette
Knitting Factory
Kori
Laparue
Layla
Le Zinc
Liquor Store Bar
Little Place
Lush
Manna
Mary Ann's
Mehanata 416 B.C.
Montrachet
Nam Phuong
Nancy Whiskey
Nino's

www.zagat.com 149

Location Index

Nobu
No Moore
Obeca Li
Odeon
Pepolino
Petite Abeille
Pico
Pig N Whistle
Puffy's Tavern
Remy Lounge
RM
Roc
Salaam Bombay
Scalini Fedeli
Screening Room
Shine
Sosa Borella
Sporting Club
Starbucks
Sugar
Sylvia Weinstock Cakes
Taylor's
Thai House Cafe
Tja!
TriBakery
Tribeca Blues
Tribeca Grand Hotel
Tribeca Grill
Tribeca Tavern
Tribeca Wine Merchants
Umanoff & Parsons
Vinyl
Walker's
Zutto

Alphabetical
Page Index

Alphabetical Page Index

Acappella	11	Bowery Ballroom	63
Aji Ichiban	105	Bridge Cafe	14, 63
Ajisen Noodle	11	Bridgewaters	107
AKA Cafe	11	Broadway Panhandler	107
Alison on Dominick Street	11	Brooklyn Bridge	137
Alleva Dairy	105	Broome Street Bar	14, 63
American Park at The Battery	11	Bubble Lounge	64
Angel	61	Bubby's	15
Angelo's of Mulberry Street	11	Burritoville	15
Anotheroom	61	Cabana Nuevo Latino	15
Antarctica	61	Cafe Colonial	15
Aquagrill	11	Cafe Gitane	64
Arlene Grocery	61	Café Habana	15
Arqua	12	Cafe Noir	15, 64
Au Mandarin	12	Caffé Roma Pastry	107
Ba Ba Malaysian	12	Canteen	15, 64
Baby Doll Lounge	61	Canton	16
Bacco	12	Capsouto Frères	16
Baked Ideas	105	Casa La Femme	16, 64
Balthazar	12, 61	Casa Mexicana	16
Balthazar Bakery	105	Castle Clinton	137
Baluchi's	12	Catherine St. Meat Market	107
Bar 89	12, 62	Ceci-Cela	107
Bari Restaurant Equip.	105	Cendrillon	16
Barocco	105	Centre Seafood	108
Barolo	13	Chanterelle	16
Barramundi	62	Charlotte's Catering	108
Barraud Caterers	106	Chez Bernard	16
Barrio	13	Chibi's Sake Bar	64
Baskin-Robbins	106	Chinatown	137
Battery Park	137	Chinatown Ice Cream	108
Battery Park City	137	Chung Chou City	108
Bayard's	13	Church Lounge	65
Bayard's Blue Bar	62	Ciao Bella Gelato	108
Bayard St. Meat Market	106	Circa Tabac	65
Bazzini, A.L., Co.	106	City Hall	17, 65
Beckett's Bar & Grill	62	City Hall and City Hall Park	137
Bell Bates Natural Food	106	Clay	17
Bereket	13	Columbine	108
Best Western Seaport Inn	132	Connecticut Muffin	108
Big Wong	13	Cosi	17
Bijoux Doux Cakes	106	Country Cafe	17
Bistro Les Amis	13	Cub Room	17, 65
Bistrot Margot	13	Culture Club	65
Blarney Stone	62	Cupping Room Cafe	17, 65
Blue Ribbon	14, 62	Cyber Cafe	65
Blue Ribbon Sushi	14	Daily Soup	17, 109
Blue Water Flowers	107	Dakota Roadhouse	66
bOb	63	Da Nico	18
Bo-Ky	14	Danube	18
Boom	63	Dean & DeLuca	109
Bot	14	Deb's	109
Botanica Bar	63	Delmonico's	18, 66
Bouley Bakery	14	Denial	66

152   www.zagat.com

Alphabetical Page Index

Dim Sum Go Go	18	Gourmet Garage	111
Dipalo Dairy	109	Governors Island	139
Diva	66	Grace	22, 69
Divine Bar	66	Grand Bar	69
Donald Sacks	66, 109	Grand Sichuan	22
Don Hill's	67	Grand Street Sausages	112
Double Happiness	67	Great NY Noodle Town	22
Doughnut Plant	109	Great Performances	112
Duane Park Cafe	18	Grilled Cheese NYC	22
Duane Park Patisserie	110	Grill Room, The	23
Dylan Prime	18, 67	G.S. Food Market	112
Ear Inn	67	Guggenheim SoHo	139
Ecco	19	Guss' Pickles	112
Economy Candy	110	Häagen Dazs	112
Edward Moran Bar & Grill	67	Hai Thanh Seafood Co.	113
Edward's	19	Hampton Chutney Co.	23
Eight Mile Creek	19, 67	Harbour Lights	23, 69
Eileen's Cheesecake	110	Harrison, The	23
Ellis Island	138	Harry's at Hanover Sq.	23, 69
El Teddy's	19, 68	Healthy Pleasures Market	113
Embassy Suites Hotel	132	Herban Kitchen	23, 113
Essex Restaurant	19	Holiday Inn Downtown	132
Evergreen Shanghai	19	Hong Kong Supermarket	113
Excellent Dumpling House	19	Honmura An	23
Famous Wines & Spirits	110	Houghtaling Mousse Pie	113
Fanelli's Cafe	20, 68	Houlihan's	24
Federal Hall	138	HSF	24
Federal Reserve Bank	138	Hudson River Club	24
Félix	20	Hung Chong Import	113
Ferrara	20, 110	Ideya	24
55 Wall	20, 68	Idlewild	70
F.illi Ponte	20	Iggy's Keltic Lounge	70
Financial District	138	Il Corallo Trattoria	24
Flor de Sol	20, 68	Il Cortile	24
Flowers of the World	111	Il Fornaio	25
Fong Inn Too	111	Il Giglio	25
Food in Motion	111	Il Palazzo	25
1492 Food	20	Independent, The	25, 70
14 Wall Street Restaurant	21	Italian Food Center	113
Fraunces Tavern	21	I Tre Merli	25, 70
Fraunces Tavern Museum	138	Ivy's Bistro	25
Full Shilling	68	Jean Claude	25
Fulton Fish Market	138	Jeremy's Ale House	70
Fun	68	Jerry's	26
Funky Broome	21	Joe's Dairy	114
Gallery, The	21	Joe's Shanghai	26
Gertel's Bake Shop	111	John Street Bar & Grill	70
Ghenet	21	Juniper Café	26
Gigino at Wagner Park	21	Kadouri & Sons	114
Gigino Trattoria	21	Kam Chueh	26
Godiva Chocolatier	111	Kam Kuo Food Corp.	114
Golden Unicorn	22	Kam Man	114
Good World Bar & Grill	22, 69	Kaña	71
Goody's	22	Katz's Delicatessen	26

www.zagat.com

Alphabetical Page Index

Kavehaz	71	Meow Mix	74
Kelley & Ping	26, 114	Mercantile Grill	74
Kin Khao	26	Merc Bar	74
Kitchen Club	27	Mercer, The	132
Kitchenette	27	Mercer Bar	75
Knitting Factory	71	Mercer Kitchen, The	30
Kori	27	Mercury Lounge	75
Kossar's Bialys	114	Mexican Radio	31, 75
Kush	71	Mezzogiorno	31
La Jumelle	71	Milady's	75
La Mela	27	Milano's Bar	75
Lansky Lounge	27, 71	Milk and Honey	75
Laparue	71	Millenium Hilton	132
Layla	27	Mint	76
L'Ecole	27	Moishe's Kosher Bake Shop	116
Le Gamin	28	Montrachet	31
Le Jardin Bistro	28	Mooza	31, 76
Leonidas	115	Motor City Bar	76
Le Pain Quotidien	28, 115	Murray's House of Beef	116
Le Père Pinard	28	Museum for African Art	139
Le Pescadou	28	Museum/Jewish Heritage	140
Le Zinc	28, 72	Ñ	31, 76
Lili's Noodle Shop & Grill	29	Naked Lunch	76
Liquor Store Bar	72	Namaskaar	31
Little Italy	139	Nam Phuong	31
Little Italy Pizza	29	Nancy Whiskey	76
Little Place, The	115	Nat. Museum/Amer. Indian	140
Living Room	72	Nello	32
Local 138	72	Neuchatel Chocolates	116
Lolita	72	Neuman & Bogdonoff	116
Lombardi's	29	New Green Bo	32
L'Orange Bleue	29, 72	New Museum/Cont. Art	140
Lotus Cafe	73	New Pasteur	32
Lower East Side	139	New York City Fire Museum	140
Lower E. Side Tenement	139	New York Marriott	133
Lucky Strike	29, 73	New York Stock Exchange	140
Ludlow Bar	73	New York Wine Exchange	117
L'Ulivo Focacceria	29	Nha Trang	32
Luna Lounge	73	Nice Restaurant	32
Lung Moon Bakery	115	Nobu	32
Lush	73	No Moore	77
Mandarin Court	29	Novecento	32
M & R Bar	73	NVBar/289 Lounge	77
Mangia	30, 115	Nyonya	33
Manhattan Bistro	30	Obeca Li	33, 77
Manna	115	Ocean Seafood	117
Mare Chiaro	74	Odeon	33, 77
Maria's Bakery	116	Oliva	33
MarkJoseph Steakhouse	30	Olive's	117
Mary Ann's	30	Omen	33
Matas Restaurant Supply	116	Once Upon a Tart	33, 117
Max Fish	74	Onieal's Grand St.	33, 77
Mehanata 416 B.C.	74	Orange Bear	77
MeKong Restaurant	30	Orchard Bar	77

154   www.zagat.com

Alphabetical Page Index

Oriental Garden	34	Savore	38
Oro Blu	34	Savoy	38, 80
Paladar	34	Scalini Fedeli	38
Pão!	34	Screening Room	38, 81
Paragon	117	71 Clinton Fresh Food	38
Paris Cafe	78	Shanghai Cuisine	39
Peasant	34, 78	Shine	81
Peking Duck House	34	Sirocco	39
Pellegrino's	34	60 Thompson	133
Penang	35	Slavin, M. & Sons, Ltd.	119
Pepe Rosso	35, 117	Slipper Room	81
Pepolino	35	Snack	39, 119
Petite Abeille	35, 117	S.O.B.'s	81
Pfiff	35	SoHo	141
Pho Bang	35	SoHo Grand Hotel	133
Pho Viet Huong	35	Soho Steak	39
Pico	36	SoHo Wines & Spirits	119
Piemonte Ravioli	118	Sosa Borella	39, 120
Pig N Whistle	78	South Street Seaport	141
Ping's Seafood	36	SouthWest NY	81
Pink Pony Cafe	78	Sporting Club	82
Pizzeria Uno Chicago	36	Spring Lounge	82
Porto Rico Importing Co.	118	Spring Street Bakery	120
Positano Ristorante	36	Spring Street Natural	39
Pravda	78	Starbucks	40
Provence	36	Staten Island Ferry	141
Puck Building	140	Statue of Liberty	141
Puck Fair	78	Stella	40
Puffy's Tavern	79	St. Maggie's Cafe	40
Quartino	36	St. Patrick's Old Cathedral	141
Raccoon Lodge	79	St. Paul's Chapel	142
Raoul's	37, 79	Streit Matzoh Co.	120
Ratner's	37	Sugar	82
Ravioli Store	118	Sullivan Street Bakery	120
Recess	79	Sway	82
Red Bench	79	Sweet & Vicious	82
Regent Wall Street	133	Sweet-n-Tart	40
Remy Lounge	79	Swim	82
Rialto	37, 80	SX 137	83
Rice	37	Sylvia Weinstock Cakes	120
Ritz-Carlton Battery Park	133	Tai Hong Lau	40
Rivertown Lounge	80	Tai Pan Bakery	121
RM	80	Taormina	41
Robert Swingle	118	Taylor's	121
Roc	37	Tennessee Mountain	41
Ron Ben-Israel Cakes	118	Ten Ren Tea	121
Room, The	80	T.G.I. Friday's	41
Roy's New York	37	Thai House Cafe	41
Ruben's Empanadas	119	Thailand Restaurant	41
Russ & Daughters	119	Thom	41
Salaam Bombay	37	Thom's Bar	83
Sal Anthony's S.P.Q.R.	38	357	83
Sammy's Roumanian	38	Tja!	41, 83
Sapphire Lounge	80	Toad Hall	83

Alphabetical Page Index

Tonic	83	Vine	43, 122
Torch	42, 84	Vintage New York	122
TriBakery	121	Vinyl	85
TriBeCa	142	Void	85
Tribeca Blues	84	Walker's	43, 86
TriBeCa Grand Hotel	134	Wall Street	142
Tribeca Grill	42, 84	Wall St. Kitchen & Bar	86
Tribeca Tavern	84	Welcome to the Johnsons	86
Tribeca Wine Merchants	121	Whiskey Ward	86
Trinity Church	142	Winnie's	86
Triple Eight Palace	42	Wo Hop	43
27 Sunrise Seafood	42	Wong Kee	43
205 Club	84	Woo Lae Oak	43
203 Spring St.	85	Woolworth Building	142
Umanoff & Parsons	121	World Financial Center	142
Va Tutto!	42	World Trade Center Site	143
Vegetarian Paradise	42	Wyanoka	43
Velvet Restaurant	85	XO Kitchen	44
Veruka	85	Yonah Schimmell's	122
Vesuvio Bakery	122	Zinc Bar	87
Vietnam	43	Zoë	44, 87
Vig Bar	85	Zutto	44